No Experience Necessary

No Experience Necessary

on-the-job training for a life of faith

Kelly A. Fryer

Augsburg
MINNEAPOLIS

NO EXPERIENCE NECESSARY
On-the-Job Training for a Life of Faith

Scripture quotations marked CEV are from the Contemporary English Version. Copyright © 1991, 1992, 1995 American Bible Society. Used by permission. Scripture quotations marked NRSV are from New Revised Standard Version Bible, copyright © 1989 Division of Christian Education of the National Council of the Churches of Christ in the United States of America. Used by permission.

Cover and book design by Gregory Washington
Back cover photo by Timothy J. Ressmeyer
Other photographic images copyright © 1999 PhotoDisc, Inc.

Library of Congress Cataloging-in-Information Data

Fryer, Kelly A., 1961-
    No experience necessary : on-the-job training for a life of faith / Fryer, Kelly A.
    p.cm.
    Includes bibliographical references.
    ISBN 0-8066-4042-1 (alk. paper)
    1. Christian life--Biblical teaching. I. Title.

    BS680.C47 F79 1999
    248.4'841--dc21

                                                                99-046723

The paper used in this publication meets the minimum requirements of American National Standard for Information Sciences—Permanence of Paper for Printed Library Materials, ANSI Z329.48-1984.

Manufactured in the U.S.A.   AF 15-8885

03   02   01   00   99   1   2   3   4   5   6   7   8   9   10

To Tim, Emma, Ethan—and the rest of my family and friends—who patiently put up with all the stories I tell about them.

A special thanks to:

- Tim Lull, who first encouraged me to use my own voice to share the story of faith—and Heather Hammond, for preserving it.
- my fellow mission pastors, who inspire me by working so hard to reach a hurting world.
- the faithful people of Immanuel, who taught me how to be a pastor—and the courageous ones at Cross of Glory who follow God wherever it leads them.

contents

preface

Before you get started . . .

I became a parent at just about the same time I was becoming a minister. These two professions have a lot in common.

First of all, you're on call twenty-four hours a day. I've been up washing pillowcases and rocking my kids to sleep at two in the morning in the middle of flu season. I've been up holding a hand and praying a prayer at two in the morning with a sad and tired family in the middle of a hospital room gone suddenly and forever quiet.

I've been called upon, in both roles, to perform tasks I was never really trained for. It's been said that, in a society where everybody specializes in something, ministers are the last true generalists. That's true, unless you count parents. I was no better prepared the first time to guide a couple through the process of getting—and staying—married than I was to have "the big talk" with my fifth grader. I did okay at both, I think, but only by the grace of God. I even managed not to choke when I heard the word *condom* come out of my ten-year-old's mouth. Nobody ever tells you beforehand that it's all going to be so hard. Who would be a mom or a dad (or a minister) if they did?

I've also needed to figure out a way to boil down the huge truths of life into something compact and portable. Instead of the whole refrigerator, I need something the size of, say, a brown paper lunch bag. I appreciate the work of scholars who do the opposite, who take simple things and pull them apart and put them back together again and end up with volumes of VERY IMPORTANT IDEAS. But I am more often faced with a four-year-old who wants to know where God lives and why those mean people hurt Jesus and why the people we love (even those who eat green vegetables) have to die. I need something to tell a forty-year-old who wants to know why his wife left him for another guy, even though he'd be willing to do whatever he could to make it work again. Really, he would.

Every single Sunday morning I stand before a diverse and demanding audience. Most of us—me included—are there because there is some big hole in our lives. And we are trusting . . . hoping . . . praying . . . wondering . . . if God can fill it. And not just any old God, either. We are there to find out what the God of Jesus Christ, the God of the Bible, has to say to us. We are there because we want the truth.

There are a lot of voices out there today offering up spiritual advice. The most crowded aisle in my local bookstore is the one lined with books promising salvation and success, hope and happiness, prosperity and peace of mind. Many of these books do not hold allegiance to any particular faith tradition but, rather, attempt to mix and match the tenets of all the world's religions, claiming those aspects that happen to appeal to the author and discarding those that do not. Some of the stuff I've read just sounds made up.

I guess I'm looking for more than that. I'm looking for answers that have stood the test of time. For truths that people have staked their lives on. I'm looking for the real thing. In my experience, the Bible will point me to it.

The Bible is the starting point of this little book. It is, in fact, THE point of this book. Each chapter is an attempt to boil down some big truth about this life—from the Bible—and apply it to real life, real people. This book won't pretend to tell the WHOLE truth—I wouldn't believe anyone out there who made such a claim—but it will make an effort to tell the honest truth, the biblical truth, about who God is and who we are and what one has to do with the other.

In the end, I'll be happy if all this book does is inspire you to pick up THE book. I hope it moves you to get up and go to the bookstore to buy yourself a Bible. Or up into the attic to dig out the one you had as a kid. If all you do is read what I have written, then you will have missed out on the greatest opportunity of your life: the chance to discover the words of the living God, written for you.

chapter 1

Strange,
but wonderful

The Bible can seem complicated and hard to understand sometimes. It might help to know that at the very center of it is this wonderful truth: GOD LOVES US. It really is as simple as that.

I have lost track of the number of people who tell me that they would like to read the Bible . . . and have TRIED to read the Bible . . . but just find it too hard to find things, much less understand them.

Among the people from whom I have heard this are teachers and stockbrokers and nurses and farmers and well, you name it. Smart people. Successful people. All of them stumped by the Bible. And most of them feel alone. Like they are the only ones in this predicament. The LAST place they would ever go is to some "Bible study" or into a bookstore that specializes in Bibles, because somebody might ask them something! And then they would have to reveal how little they know.

Well, I'm not going to kid you. Reading the Bible really can be hard work. There are people and places and issues in it that are just totally foreign to the average reader today. We'll sort through some of them together later on.

But you know, it can be surprisingly easy to read the Bible, too. Sometimes, miraculously easy! Even in the beginning, you'll be reading along, and suddenly you'll GET IT. The truth will emerge as clearly as your reflection in the bathroom mirror as the steam from your shower is toweled away. In stunned silence, you know the words you have just read were meant for you. And you SEE yourself. Then you'll know this Bible isn't just a lot of old dead sayings. There's life in those words!

It is not God's intention to keep the truth hidden from us. The Bible, after all, is the written account of what God has to say. God is actively trying to communicate with us through these words. And the single most important thing that God is trying to say is this: YOU ARE LOVED.

Kind of a Strange Message

At the center of the Bible is this wonderful truth: God loves us. God loves us even though we don't always deserve it. Even when we don't believe it. Even when we can't love ourselves. God loves us without condition, without hesitation. God loves us enough to lay down the law about how to live so that we can find peace and happiness forever. And God loves us enough to give us another chance when we mess it up the first two million times. God's heart is full of nothing but love for us, through no effort of our own. It really is as simple as that.

But I won't blame you if you have a hard time believing it.

Our local Better Business Bureau ran an ad in the yellow pages a few years ago giving this advice: If something looks too good to be true, it probably is. Most of us learn this lesson early. I learned it in the alley behind my house the first time I tried to ride a bike. It seemed like all of my friends learned how to do it before I did. My bike, a beautiful new Schwinn with streamers hanging from the handlebars and a blue banana seat, arrived on Christmas morning. By springtime I was anxious to take it for a ride. It was harder than it looked. I still have the scars on my knees to prove it.

A lot of things in this life are too good to be true. That's what I tell those starry-eyed couples when they come to ask me to marry them and they say they've never had a fight. Just wait, I say, with a knowing smile. It's been awhile since I put the dents in our frying pan. But I am reminded of how hard my husband and I have had to work for what we have every single time I scramble an egg.

The central truth of the Bible, though, is too good NOT to be true: Becoming a child of God really is the easiest thing you'll ever do. In fact, there is NOTHING you have to do. It is a gift. I think it's kind of funny, really, that in a world where most things worth having take so darn much work, becoming a child of God takes none at all.

Bob

The first time I realized how important—and how difficult—it is for us to understand the wonderful message at the center of the Bible came in the middle of my first month on the job. A handful of people were sitting around the table, most of them more scared than I was. They were sitting there because I was supposed to be teaching them about what it means to be a follower of Jesus. They were new members and, at that church, it was assumed that if you were a "new" one you couldn't possibly know as much as the "old" ones. So I was in the middle of talking about God's grace, which was where they told us in seminary we should always begin.

I was saying that grace works something like this: It's your first day of school. And you're nervous and shy and feeling completely inadequate. You're wondering whether or not you can cut it when suddenly the teacher walks in, looks over, and says to the whole class, "You all get A's." Before you've done or said or accomplished or messed up anything! "Now," the teacher says with a smile, "just do your best." That, I told my class, is sort of what grace is like. GOD LOVES YOU BEFORE YOU EVEN DO ANYTHING TO DESERVE IT.

Now, I didn't make up this example of grace myself, although I can't remember where I first heard it. And it's not the best one I've ever used. In fact, it's really quite ordinary. But, when I told THAT story THIS time, something wonderful happened.

I looked up across the table and I saw Bob. He was thirty-something, the owner of a moderately successful small business, the father of three. He actually had tears in his eyes. They were piling up on the very rim of his eye and threatening to spill over right down his face. In public and all. "What's up, Bob?" I said in my blurt-it-out-and-hope-it-doesn't-backfire sort of way. And he said this: "I don't think I ever knew who God was before."

God Wants You Anyway

"I don't think I ever knew who God was . . ."

It's amazing to me, although it shouldn't be, that for many people today those words are true. Like most of the people I know, I grew up thinking that God's job was to make life HARD for us: "Do this" and especially "Don't do that." God took all the fun out of everything, we thought. God expects us to be perfect. God's angry because we're not. We'll never measure up. Some of us have driven ourselves crazy trying, collapsing finally in despair at the hopelessness of it all. Others of us convinced ourselves at some point that we were among the few who managed to do it, to reach the mark, to meet God's unyielding standards. And we've succeeded in making everybody else around us crazy with our fantastic arrogance.

That second group—the arrogant ones—probably wouldn't like to hear me put it this way, but the truth of the matter is, Jesus has never been very choosy. He doesn't look for a diploma hanging on your wall. He doesn't much care what your bank account balance is. Or if you can balance it at all. He isn't much interested in your wardrobe or your waistline or your annual winter vacation destination. I'm not the only one who finds it sort of funny that, when we go to church on Sunday morning, we usually pull out our best clothes to wear—"Sunday finest"—and all

God loves you before you even do anything to deserve it.

that. And if we don't, because we're just sick and tired of dressing up for work every day, we feel a little guilty about it. Truth is, none of those things matter to Jesus.

In the Bible the people who mattered most to Jesus were the ones who needed him most. The messy. The ugly. The ones who never quite made it. It is still that way, I think. One day a few years ago I got a call from a guy who runs a group home for disabled adults. He asked if it would be okay for the residents of his home to come to our church. I said, "Of course. But, why are you *asking* me?" He said, "Well, some churches have said no."

It's easy to get mixed up. We figure, I guess, that if the world values something or someone, then God must value them, too. And I guess we figure the opposite is also true. But Jesus wasn't like that. Not even close.

I think that's one of the reasons he had so many people— sometimes thousands of them—following him wherever he went. He just wandered around the countryside issuing a simple invitation: "Come with me."[1] And, along the way, he picked up an unlikely group of followers and friends: fishermen and tax collectors and housewives. Rumor had it there was even a prostitute or two in the bunch.

[1]Luke 5:1-11, 27-28 CEV

Jesus is not the Marine Corps. He is not looking for a few good men. Or women. He is looking for YOU. He knows all about you. And he wants you anyway. He knows about that test you cheated on in fourth grade. And that time you cheated on your taxes back in 1983. And that time you were one drink away from cheating on your wife. He knows about my flying frying pan incident. He knows it all. And he wants you anyway. He wants me too.

Becoming a child of God is the easiest thing you'll ever do. That is THE central message, the number one truth, of the Bible.

This Is How It Works

Becoming a child of God is so easy because, in fact, Jesus has already done it all for you. That's what the Bible says, anyway. That was the whole point of Jesus dying on the cross: so that you and I might live life as forgiven children of God! I believe it. I really do. But there is a difference between BELIEVING something and understanding it. To be honest, I've always had a hard time understanding this.

That early missionary, Paul, tried to explain to his friends what difference the death of Jesus made to them. We still have some of his letters. We can read how the cross of Jesus was God's ultimate way of proving he loves us. And why Jesus' death was the most important thing that ever happened to us. This is what Paul said: "But God was merciful! We were dead because of our sins, but God loved us so much that he made us alive with Christ, and God's wonderful kindness is what saves you . . . You were saved by faith in God, who treats us much better than we deserve."[2]

Read those words again, if you didn't pay attention the first time. They are beautiful words. They speak right to my heart.

[2]Ephesians 2:4-5, 8 CEV

But my head is another story entirely. My head is going, "What in the heck does that mean???" WHY did Jesus have to die to do all that? How does it work, anyway? Couldn't God have thought of some other way? I mean, Hallmark is pretty good at coming up with the right words, for ANY occasion. Couldn't God have just sent a card—HEY DOWN THERE . . . I LOVE YOU! Or something like that? You can send an e-card for free, for goodness' sake!

I don't know. Maybe it's just me.

But just in case you're the same way and ask the same kinds of questions and wonder what the point of the cross really was, I want to pass on to you a story that I heard that helped me make sense of it all. It is called "The Accident":

A little child is playing ball on a quiet neighborhood street. Predictably, the ball bounces out in the middle of the street and, without looking, the child chases it. In the meantime, a truck is barreling down that very same street. The driver is speeding, without regard to anyone or anything else.

You know what is going to happen next. The squealing tires. A mother's scream. And then, a silence so awful that no siren and no sermon can ever fill it.

The most terrible tragedy imaginable is about to happen. But then, suddenly . . . amazingly . . . miraculously . . . a man appears. Just an ordinary man. A passerby. A stranger with every excuse in the world not to get involved. A man who could not, however, just stand by and watch.

It takes not more than a moment for him to act. He doesn't even think about it. Without regard for his own life, he jumps in front of the truck and pushes the child out of the way. The child, thank God, is saved.

But the man who saved the child is killed.[3]

---

[3]Gerhard O. Forde used this example in *Christian Dogmatics* (ed. Carl E. Braaten and Robert W. Jenson, Philadelphia, Fortress Press, 1984, vol. 2, 7th locus, 88-89).

When I first heard that story I realized right away, of course, that the man who made that sacrifice was supposed to be Jesus. And I thought that my place in the story was also clear. "I am the child," I thought. "Jesus, thank God, saved me." I bet that's what you are thinking, too.

But go with me here for a minute. As I survey the horrible scene in the street I realize I am looking out through the windshield and into the eyes of that stranger who gave up his life. Slowly it dawns on me that I am not the child at all. I am, more truthfully, the driver of that truck.

I barrel through life selfishly, without regard for the welfare or the needs of others. I might not throw frying pans anymore, but I still want what I want when I want it. And believe me, I throw plenty of words around that hurt even more than a frying pan ever could. I am not proud of this, mind you. Not at all. I KNOW I should live . . . think . . . act . . . better. I even give it a good try most of the time. But I still come home after a bad day and feel like kicking something.

But even as the truck driver, my life too has been saved. Selfish as I might be. Stupid as I sometimes am. In spite of everything I have ever been or done or thought about. In spite of it all, a man with every excuse in the world not to notice and not to care gives his life for me. He throws himself in my path and rescues me from my own self-destruction. He gives me a chance to live another day. He gives me a chance to change my ways. Jesus, thank God, has saved me too.

This is how it works. When we become children of God it is not by our own effort. It is not even because we deserve it. In fact, we COULDN'T deserve it. We could never do enough to earn a place in God's heart. God, after all, IS perfect. And we could never be. But we ARE God's children, loved and cherished, forgiven and given a place in God's heart, invited to live with God forever. Why? Simple. Because God loves us. And because Jesus has sacrificed himself for us. Before we can do a single thing to help or prove or defend ourselves, God plants an A+ right on our foreheads and right on our hearts.

It really is that easy. Thanks, Bob, for reminding me.

GETTING INTERESTED?
More Reading You Can Do

- **John 8:1-11** This is the story of a woman who had everything going against her. She was a woman, first of all, living at a time when women were not granted even the most fundamental rights or respect. And she had been caught in the act of adultery. In the ACT, the story says. The story doesn't say where the guy was. But this woman was getting the worst of it. She was about to be stoned to death when, all of a sudden, Jesus showed up. He rescued her. He made a career of that back then. Still does. What do you need rescuing from?

- **Romans 5:1-21** This is tough reading. But it's worth it. Try reading it a couple of times. Underline the parts you think are important, the parts that speak to YOU. (Here are some definitions that might help you figure out what Paul is talking about. *Justified:* brought into alignment—made right with—God. *Grace:* God's unconditional, never-failing love, which forgives us and gives us peace! *Righteous:* holy and whole. *Sinner:* ALL of us, because we instinctively turn away from following God's path for our lives and go our own way. *Reconciled:* see *justified* above!)

GETTING PERSONAL:
Some Things to Think About

- IF YOU DON'T ALREADY HAVE A SPIRITUAL JOURNAL, START ONE TODAY.

- Give this some thought: What selfish, stupid things have you done lately? Open up and talk to God about them; write them down in your journal. Ask God to forgive you. He already knows all about them, you know. That's why he sent Jesus.

- Jesus is giving you a second chance today. How will you use it? What things would you like to do differently? What areas of your life need to be changed? Use your journal to make a list of them. Ask God to help make it so.

- If you never knew what God was like before, you might be wondering how to respond to the Savior who has been loving you and waiting for you all this time. You can start by saying "Thank you." Do it now. But what God really wants is for you to place your life in Jesus' hands. Here is a prayer to get you started:

Jesus, I believe you offered your life for mine. I trust that you died on the cross to give me a new life free of guilt and fear. Starting now, I will answer your invitation to live in relationship with you, receiving your love and sharing it with others. I want to be your follower. I want the peace and the wholeness and the joy that only you can bring. Help me to follow you, Jesus, all the days of my life. Amen

GETTING SERIOUS:
A Bible Verse to Memorize

You were saved by faith in God, who treats us much better than we deserve. This is God's gift to you, and not anything you have done on your own. Ephesians 2:8 CEV

chapter 2

when
GOD
aches

At the center of the Bible is the wonderful message that God loves us even when we don't deserve it. The flip side of that, of course, is that we usually don't.

It all started, like so many childhood disasters, with a baseball. It was a baseball that gave my little brother his first concussion. A baseball gave me my first lesson in life's injustices: they wouldn't let me play on a REAL team because I was a girl. No matter that my pitching arm was the best in the neighborhood.

I was also a pretty good hitter, which is how we got in so much trouble that day. My brother threw it. I hit it, right through his bedroom window. My dad was surprisingly calm about the whole thing. He brought the ball out into the yard, having recovered it from wherever it landed. We didn't actually see where it landed because we were hiding behind the garage praying for the power of invisibility. When he found us he gave us the ball back and asked us not to play baseball in the yard anymore. It was a pretty small yard and we were getting a lot better at the game. We took the ball. Dad went to the hardware store. The window was fixed by suppertime.

What happened the next day is rather less clear. I said it was my brother's fault. He blamed me. My dad didn't seem to care. There was that same troublesome little ball, lying in the middle of a pile of glass, in the middle of my brother's bedroom, having smashed its way through the very same window. Dumb, I know. This time my dad was in the backyard, spherical evidence in hand, before we could even take cover. He sent us to our rooms. To wait.

I was only about eight years old, but every second of my short little life flashed before my eyes as I sat on my bed and waited for my dad's wrath to descend upon me. I deserved every bit of it. And I knew it. But that only made the waiting that much worse.

In some ways, every good deed I've done ever since has been an effort to avoid ever feeling that bad again. Guilt can be a terrible thing if we hang on to it long after God and everybody else has gotten over whatever it is we've done. But guilt can be a really good thing, too, when it pushes us to see where we've gone wrong.

Anyway, my dad must have seen the guilty dread in my face. He had come in to deliver a spanking, which was as about as creative as a lot of parents got back then when it came to disciplining their kids. But it never got past the token stage. And he even had a hard time doing that. "This hurts me more than it hurts you," he said.

I didn't really believe that, of course. Not until I had kids of my own. Kids who—as wonderful as they are and as hard as we've tried to help them avoid it—have made their share of mistakes and will make plenty more. Now I know what my dad was talking about when he said "This hurts me more." And it wasn't the token spanking he doled out that day, either.

It really DOES hurt us when we see our kids messing up.

It hurts most when we can't fix it for them, the way we could when a Band-Aid would do the trick. It is a terrible thing to have to watch as our kids answer for their mistakes, to have to stand by as they endure punishment they might otherwise have been able to avoid. We hurt for our kids even before they get hurt because we can anticipate the trouble they're in for. Our kids don't usually understand the seriousness of their actions. They have no idea. But we do. We can see it coming. It's as clear to us as . . . well . . . as clear as that brand new window was the second time my dad replaced it.

God Aches for Us When We Get Lost

I am convinced this is how it is with God, too.

I believe that God aches for us when we get ourselves lost and into trouble. God loves us always, of course, but God loves us the most when we are really in a mess. God has a special place in his heart for sinners. This is why Jesus ate with them all the time. We know he did because that was one of the things that got him into the most hot water. The Pharisees and the scribes, and other religious elitists were always grumbling about it. "This man is friendly with sinners. He even eats with them," they complained.[1]

For some reason, how to eat was a big deal back then. There were all kinds of rules about how to do it. About what to eat. And what not to eat. And who to eat with. And who to stay clear of. These were religious rules. They weren't made up by Weight Watchers or the Surgeon General. The idea was that sinners were UNCLEAN, people you wouldn't want in your house or at your table, for fear of offending the Almighty. Jesus knew better.

Jesus went out looking for people like that to have dinner with. He was at his best when he was looking across the table and over his pita bread at somebody who just yesterday was on

[1]Luke 15:2 CEV

the outside looking in. One of these poor souls, a tax collector named Levi, threw a big party for Jesus. Invited all his unpopular, tax-collecting friends. These were guys who not only made a living collecting legitimate taxes people owed the government—which would be unpopular enough—but who extorted an additional share for themselves. These thieving cheats robbed from the poor and gave to themselves. By the end of the day, Levi was one of the twelve apostles. Part of Jesus' inner circle. Jesus' friend. We know him better now as Matthew.[2]

What Jesus showed us again and again is that, to God, a sinner is not necessarily mean or unclean. A sinner is not even somebody who breaks a bunch of rules (or windows!) although sinners do that. In fact, sin is not really about RULES at all. It is simpler than that. Sin is about breaking off our RELATIONSHIP with God and choosing to go it alone. A sinner is somebody who tells God in effect "Go away! I, me, and mine are all I want or need." A sinner is somebody who wanders off into a self-centered wilderness, chasing after her own whims. Again. And again. No matter how much trouble she got herself (or others) into the first two million times she did it. A sinner ends up disappointed and empty-handed. God aches when that happens. I am a sinner. You are too. Although it wouldn't surprise me if it made you mad that I said so.

Sin has been given kind of a bum rap lately. It is too negative, I guess, for the feel-good culture we live in. Self-help books and talk show hosts encourage us to find the light within and just be our wonderful, true selves. Mention sin and they'll tell you to find a good therapist. They're missing the whole point. Apart from God we don't HAVE a wonderful, true self!

[2]Luke 5:27-32 Matthew—or someone from his group of friends—eventually wrote down the story of Jesus. That story is in our Bible as "The Gospel according to Matthew." Jesus was thinking ahead when he called this tax collector—a good record-keeper, after all!—to follow him!

Some part of us has always known that. But instead of turning to God (the One and Only) we make up our own. We make gods for ourselves. We make gods of ourselves. We invent puny, tiresome little gods like money or comfort or making it to the top of whatever heap we've set our heart on. We stupidly look inside ourselves for truth and light, instead of listening to God, who IS truth, and looking to God, who IS light.

God hates it when we do that. Because God knows how much danger we are in when we do.

Here's an example of the kind of trouble we can get into when we wander off on our own: There is a part of Ireland not on any tourist map I am aware of. How I got there and where I thought I was going, I can't really say. It is a desolate place called Connemara. Not a single car passed by for at least five hours. I had been hiking through the rocky, barren countryside for quite awhile before I noticed the sheep. Wild-eyed sheep, ready to charge and attack anything that moved. The police officers who finally came by and gave me a lift out of there told me those sheep were crazy. Literally. They had wandered off at some point and gotten lost. Maybe somewhere in their foolish sheep's brains they figured they could take care of themselves. Who needs a shepherd, with those big shears? But their overgrown, matted wool became a breeding place for some sort of parasite. This parasite infected their brains. So now life—their lives—consisted of scavenging food among the rocks, becoming a terror to themselves, and scaring silly college kids half to death.

There is probably some technical, veterinary explanation for what I saw. I don't need it. The Bible says "all of us were like sheep that had wandered off."[3] Bad things happen to sheep (and to people) when they go wandering off on their own without a clue. I saw it in Connemara. I see it in the world around me, in the newspaper, and on TV. I have seen it in my own life.

And, just like Dad, God has seen it coming from a mile away.

[3]Isaiah 53:6 CEV

God Rejoices When We Are Found Again

When the religious leaders pressed Jesus on this eating thing, he tried to explain why it was he was so willing to sit with sinners and welcome them. He, too, had a sheep story to explain it. "If any of you has a hundred sheep, and one of them gets lost, what will you do? Won't you leave the ninety-nine in the field and go look for the lost sheep until you find it? And when you find it, you will be so glad that you will put it on your shoulder and carry it home."[4] In other words, the God whose heart breaks when we do dumb and dangerous things is filled with joy when we turn it around. As racked with sorrow as God is when we get lost, God is that much more glad when we are found. God hates it when we put ourselves or others in danger because of the foolish choices we make. But God rejoices when we let ourselves be led back home again.

The Pharisees and the scribes still didn't get it. I can't say I blame them. That sheep Jesus was talking about was just plain stupid! Wandering off into a wild place where wolves and deadly cliffs await. Making the shepherd leave the rest of the flock alone, unattended, afraid. Putting itself and the rest of them in danger. But Jesus said the shepherd, when he found the lost sheep, put it up on his shoulders and carried it back to safety. Gently. Smiling. Me? I'd be kicking it! Poking it along with my big old shepherd's crook.

No one is so lost that God can't find them.

Hard. "Get back to the flock, you stupid sheep," I'd be saying. "What were you THINKING?!? Do you have ANY idea how much trouble you could've gotten yourself into?!? What is the MATTER with you?!?" Not Jesus. Saving stupid, silly sheep who go wandering off into danger is what he came for.

[4]Luke 15:4-6a CEV

Later on in the story we find out that these religious leaders, the Pharisees and scribes, help get Jesus killed.[5] They didn't like what Jesus had to say to them about sheep and sinners at the dinner table that day. They figured, I guess, that once you're lost you stay lost. You probably deserve to be, too. So there. Which is kind of ironic when you think about it, because it is in the cross of Jesus that God shows us once and for all: No one is so lost that God can't find them.

Jesus did a lot of other stuff while he was down here, but none of it was more important than this. He came to bring home the lost ones. He came to bring sinners back to God. He came to forgive the unforgivable. He came to love.

In fact, one of the very last things Jesus did was to reach out and rescue someone. When they put Jesus on the cross, he was not alone. At least two others were put to death that awful day. One on either side of him. They were criminals. And according to one of them, anyway, whatever they had done had earned them this death sentence. They deserved to be where they were. One of them couldn't get past himself enough to see what Jesus had to offer. But the other did. "Remember me, Jesus!" he said. "Remember me when you get to heaven!" He wouldn't have dared to ask Jesus to TAKE him there. He was a sinner, after all. Deserving of death. He had made a real mess of everything. And he knew that God knew it. God knows everything. But Jesus knew all about God. And God loves sinners. "I'll tell you what," Jesus said, "I won't have to remember you when I get to heaven. Because, today, you're coming with me!"[6]

This is what Jesus came here for. To rescue those who know that, without him, they don't stand a chance. That letter-writer, Paul, tried to explain this to his friends in Rome. "Christ died for us at a time when we were helpless and sinful. No one is

---

[5]Luke 23:10
[6]Chapters 22 and 23 of Luke tell the story of Jesus' last supper, betrayal, arrest, and death. Read it. He did it all for you.

really willing to die for an honest person, though someone might be willing to die for a truly good person. But God showed how much he loved us by having Christ die for us, even though we were sinful."[7] Jesus didn't come to earth, you see, because we were all so perfect. Jesus came because we weren't. And because God will stop at nothing to show his love for us. Jesus came to rescue us from every danger, especially the danger we put ourselves in.

Now, I know this goes against every experience we have ever had. You see, I do it too. I'm driving down the road and some jer . . . ur . . . misguided and obviously harried individual . . . cuts me off going twenty miles over the speed limit. I usually don't honk or shake my fist at him. But under my breath I say, "I hope you get yours, buddy."

That's how we've set things up down here, in our world. Troublemakers are supposed to get what's coming to them. Wrongdoers get punished. That's what we call justice. That's why the result of a broken window is a spanking, no matter how token, or a grounding or, at the very least, a good long lecture. That's what we're used to.

I can't remember where I heard this story, but it's a classic: Late for a very important meeting, a driver parks his car illegally and leaves this note, "I have circled this block for twenty minutes and now I'm late for my appointment. If I don't park here I'll lose my job. FORGIVE US OUR TRESPASSES." When he returned he found a ticket on his windshield and a note, "I've circled this block for twenty years. If I don't give you this ticket, I'll lose my job. LEAD US NOT INTO TEMPTATION."

That's our world. And there is not a lot of leeway in it. There is not a very big margin for error. If you're lost, you probably deserve to be. So there.

No wonder the Pharisees didn't get it.

[7]Romans 5:6-8 CEV

What Jesus came to show us was something the world had never seen before. He put it like this: "There is more happiness in heaven because of one sinner who turns to God than over ninety-nine good people who don't need to."[8]

Yeah. As if there are ninety-nine people like THAT out there somewhere.

GETTING INTERESTED?
More Reading You Can Do

- **Luke 15** This whole chapter contains one wonderful story after another describing our loving God. Read these stories over and over again until they are a part of your very being. Use your journal to write your own version of these stories. Paraphrase them. Put them in your own words. Know them well enough that you can tell them to somebody else, somebody who needs to hear them.
- **Acts 9** Saul was mighty tough on Christians before he met Jesus; it was his job, in fact, to hunt down those early Christians and kill them! He never got over the way God forgave him. In fact, he eventually became "Paul," the greatest Christian missionary ever! How can you relate to Paul? What huge sin has God forgiven you for?
- **1 Timothy 1:12-17** Here Paul himself tells what it meant to him to be so loved by God; it changed his life forever. How has your life been changed by God so far? What other changes would you like to see?

GETTING PERSONAL:
Some Things to Think About

- Where are you in your spiritual life? Are you on the path that God has laid out before you? Or are you wandering

[8]Luke 15:7 CEV

around in the wilderness? Use your journal to describe where you are, spiritually, right now.

- Have you experienced the love and forgiveness of God? Tell somebody about it today!
- If you haven't experienced God's forgiveness, ask God for it right now. Use this prayer or one of your own:
  Dear God, I am sorry for having wandered away from you. Forgive me. And put me back on the right path. Help me to follow you. Amen

GETTING SERIOUS:
A Bible Verse to Memorize

God showed his love for us when he sent his only Son into the world to give us life. 1 John 4:9 CEV

chapter 3

No experience necessary

Okay, so the Bible has a little something to say about who God is. And about who WE are. Want more? Let's go!

Did you know that the Bible has been the world's number one best-selling book every single year since the year it was published? I heard that somewhere and I guess I believe it. But you would think that with all those Bibles out there EVERYBODY would know EVERYTHING there is to know about God.

I don't really know why they don't. Is it because the Bible is such a very old book that everybody assumes there's nothing worth reading in there anymore? Or is it because they don't know where to begin? Maybe it's because reading the Bible takes at least a little work and a little patience and we are people who want what we want RIGHT NOW and are too overworked and too tired to put much effort into anything. I don't know.

But I do know that the Bible shows us a God who loves us. And helps us see how badly we NEED a God like that. And I know that this is only the beginning. The Bible promises to lead us into a lifetime of learning and growing.

If you're looking for more . . . if you really want to hear what God is saying to you through the words of the Bible . . . if you're hoping and praying that the God of the Bible can lead you into a life of hope and peace and joy . . . try the following basic principles.

Read It Like a Tom Clancy Novel

I'm not kidding. That is the single best piece of advice I can give you when it comes to opening up the Bible. Read it like a good book. Because that, after all, is what the Bible is.

Now, you do need to be prepared when you open up this particular book. The biblical writers (and there are many of them, which we'll get to later) were all trying to be as clear as they could be. They WANTED their readers to know exactly what they were trying to say about God and the world and people's place in it all. But that doesn't mean there won't be moments when you feel frustrated and confused. There will, I'm sure, be places you don't recognize. There will be references you don't catch to customs and cultural realities you don't know anything about. There will be people you don't know, whose names you can't even pronounce. There will—especially toward the front of the book—be lists of rules and regulations so long, written for people so long ago, that you'll wonder for a moment what EVER made you think reading this book would be a good idea in the first place.

Well, relax. And don't worry too much about all the things you don't understand or don't really care about. At least in the beginning. Just try reading it like a Tom Clancy novel.

I love adventure books. The political intrigue and the spy stuff and so on. Plus Mr. Clancy creates great characters. And I can picture Harrison Ford when I read because he has played Clancy's most famous character, Jack Ryan, in the movies. You've got to love any book that can give you Harrison Ford in the privacy of your own imagination. That is what I do on my vacations. But I have had to overcome one small problem in order to enjoy these books. Clancy fills his novels with all kinds of technical language and military slang that I don't know anything about. Listen to this:

" 'Two new contacts, sir, designate Sierra Twenty and Twenty-one. Both appear to be submerged contacts. Sierra Twenty, bearing three-two-five, direct path and faint . . . stand by . . . okay, looks like a Han-class SSN, good cut on the fifty-Hertz line, plant noise also. Twenty-one, also submerged contact, at three-three-zero, starting to look like a Xia, sir.'

" 'A boomer in a FleetEx?' the senior chief wondered."[1]

I have a friend, believe it or not, who reads Clancy novels BECAUSE of this kind of stuff. He's an engineer, of course, and a techno-geek. He loves the real live lingo and the references to all the latest, greatest technological achievements. Me? I read these books IN SPITE of this stuff. I read them because they tell a good story and because I care about the characters. And somehow, I manage to get the point—even though the technical language goes right over my head.

It isn't much different, for those of us who are not Bible experts or history buffs or theology professors, when we sit down to read the stories in the Bible. Some of the technical language is going to go right over our heads. Odds are, when you start reading, you are going to have no idea who most of the people are. And you're going to be clueless about the historical context. And the geography? Well, forget it. I don't know where a lot of other countries are on the map TODAY, much less four thousand years ago.

But you know what? It doesn't matter. Really. At least not in the beginning.

When you sit down with the Bible, read it for the story. It will be even more exciting than a Clancy novel because, in this

---

[1]Tom Clancy, *Executive Orders* (New York: G. P. Putnam's Sons, 1996), 373.

case, the story is true! And read it because you care about the characters. You will soon discover that one of the most important characters in the biblical story is you.

Know the Basics

Now, once you're all settled in to read this good book, it WILL help to know a few of the basics.

Start with knowing how to find your way around the Bible. First, every Bible is divided into two main sections called the Old Testament and the New Testament. (Some Bibles also include something called the Apocrypha, a section you might find at the end of the book, that contains ancient writings considered valuable and worthwhile by Christians but that didn't make it into the official list of writings accepted by all Christians.) Second, both the Old Testament and the New Testament are divided into books. Each book is divided into chapters. And within each chapter are numbered verses. The chapters and verses are numbered exactly the same in every version of the Bible, universally, in every language.

Once you understand how it works, you can find any Bible passage with relative ease. For example, if you were to look up

---

The Resurrection of Jesus
(Mt 28.1–10; Mk 16.1–8; Jn 20.1–10)

24 But on the first day of the week, at early dawn, they came to the tomb, taking the spices that they had prepared. 2 They found the stone rolled away from the tomb, 3 but when they went in, they did not find the body.[n] 4 While they were perplexed about this, suddenly two men in dazzling clothes stood beside them. 5 The women[o] were terrified and bowed their faces to the ground, but the men[p] said to them, "Why do you look for the living among the dead? He is not here, but has risen.[q] 6 Remember how he told you, while he was still in Galilee, 7 that the Son of Man must be handed over to sinners, and be crucified, and on the third day rise again." 8 Then they remembered his words 9 and turning from the tomb

the one to redeem Israel.[v] Yes, and besides all this, it is now the third day since these things took place. 22 Moreover, some women of our group astounded us. They were at the tomb early this morning, 23 and when they did not find his body there, they came back and told us that they had indeed seen a vision of angels who said that he was alive. 24 Some of those who were with us went to the tomb and found it just as the women had said; but they did not see him." 25 Then he said to them, "Oh, how foolish you are and how slow of heart to beli and how the prophets have 26 Was it not necessary th siah[w] should then

---

Luke 24:2-3, you would first look for the book called Luke
in the table of contents. You would find it listed in the New
Testament. Once in the book of Luke, you would turn to chapter 24—usually marked with a large, bold number. Finally, you
would look for the verses, marked with smaller numbers, 2 and 3.

Something that may surprise you is that the Bible is actually
a collection of books. But they were written by many different
people over the course of centuries. Let me tell you a little more
about the two sections of the Bible called the Old Testament
and the New Testament.

The Old Testament

This part of the Bible tells the story of God's relationship with
the Hebrew people in the centuries before Jesus was born. It
was, in fact, originally written in Hebrew. Many different
authors have contributed to the books of the Old Testament,
each attempting to capture the oral traditions and stories of this
ancient people in writing. This took time. In fact, some scholars
suggest that more than a thousand years passed between the
time the earliest and the latest passages were written down.
It is hard to pinpoint exactly when the final form of the Old
Testament was established, but it most likely happened before
the year 200 B.C.

As you can imagine, the thousand-year history of an ancient
people is a colorful one. There are wars and famines. There are
scoundrels and saviors, tyrants and thieves, nomads and farmers.
There is slavery and deliverance. Babies are born and kings are
made and friends are betrayed. These stories are conveyed in
historical accounts and wise sayings, prayers and poems and
songs. There are even a few long lists of rules and regulations
that helped these long-ago people live together peacefully, in
good health. There is no shortage of adventure.

The Old Testament begins with a history of God's relationship to humankind. In the first five books (Genesis, Exodus,

Leviticus, Numbers, and Deuteronomy) of the Old Testament, the stories of creation are found, along with a series of agreements or promises made between God and the people of the world. These books describe the special relationship established between God and the Hebrew people. God—and God's will for the world—is revealed through the history of the Hebrews, the people of Israel.

It is in the Old Testament that you find many of the greatest stories of all time. Adam and Eve are in here. So are Noah and his ark, Moses and the Ten Commandments, David and Goliath, Daniel and the lions' den, King Solomon and the Proverbs, Jonah and the whale. The prophets are here: Isaiah, Jeremiah, Ezekiel, and several more. These stories gave Charlton Heston his start in the movies and have been keeping Hollywood busy ever since.

The main thing to understand is that the stories of the Old Testament reveal a God who is full of power and glory, but who is also rich in mercy. A God who loves us! Enough to lay down the law. The God we meet in the Old Testament is the God who gave us Ten Commandments (Exodus 20) and who shows us time and again how to walk in holiness and peace. God wants good things for us and shows us the way. This is how God describes, through the prophet Moses, what is required from all his people—here called Israel: "Listen, Israel! The LORD our God is the only true God! So love the LORD your God with all your heart, soul, and strength."[2]

When we wander away from the path God has set before us, causing harm to ourselves, God is broken-hearted. And God is absolutely furious when we make idiotic and disastrous choices that cause harm to others. But, even in anger, God is merciful and willing to give us the opportunity to start again. God is faithful to us, no matter how stubborn or stupid we have been. God never turns away from us. This is the God we meet

[2]Deuteronomy 6:4-5 CEV

in the ancient stories of the Old Testament: a God who never breaks a promise.

The New Testament

The New Testament is the story of how God kept the most important promise of all, that a Savior would be sent for all the people of the world. This Messiah would rescue them from darkness and death, and deliver them from their own worst impulses, and put them back on the path of life. Christians believe God fulfilled that promise in the person of Jesus Christ.

The New Testament was written in Greek, the predominant language of that time. It begins with four books, called gospels. Each gospel was written by a different person. They all include stories from the life of Jesus. They describe miracles he performed, sermons he delivered, people he met, his death, and his resurrection. The four gospel writers are known as Matthew, Mark, Luke, and John. Some of these writers were actually on the scene, eyewitnesses to the events that took place during the life of Jesus. Others experienced these events through the first-hand reports given them by actual witnesses. Each writer describes these events from a unique perspective. The result is that some of the details of the story differ from book to book. There is complete agreement among the four writers about the one most important thing: that Jesus of Nazareth is the long-awaited Messiah, the Son of God, the Savior of the world. This is the good news that each of the New Testament writers intends for us to read in their stories. They want us to hear good news for our lives in the story of Jesus Christ. In fact, the word *gospel* is an Old English word that means "good news"!

Following the four gospels is a collection of books that includes letters written by the leaders of the early Christian church. The biggest letter-writer of all was a man named Paul.

Paul traveled around starting new churches and, as he moved, he would keep in touch with the friends he had made by writing letters to them. In his letters he would continue to teach them about Jesus. He also filled his letters with practical advice about how the Christian faith might impact their family life, marriages, work life, church life, and so on. Of the many letters he wrote, the Bible preserves the ones he wrote to the communities of Christians who lived during the decades following Jesus' death and resurrection in the ancient cities of Rome, Corinth, Galatia, Ephesus, Philippi, Colossae, and Thessalonica.

You can find Paul's own story in the book of Acts, which gives the history of the early Christian community, beginning in chapter 9. Paul is a guy many of us can relate to. He started out thinking Christians and this Jesus fellow they worshiped were crazy. Dangerous, even. He had made it his own personal mission to hunt down bands of new Christians and have them put to death. In fact, he was on his way to do just that in a town called Damascus when he ran into the risen Jesus. Well, actually, Jesus spoke to him out of a light so bright it blinded him and knocked him right off his high horse. Literally. "What in the world do you think you're doing?" Jesus asked him. And that was pretty much all Jesus had to say. Once Paul got up and his eyesight finally came back, he started singing a different tune. And he sang it well. No one ever did a better job of getting the word out about Jesus than Paul did. You'll see what I mean when you read the rest of Acts.

The book of Acts, together with the letters that follow it, describe what happened in the early church after the living Jesus departed earth and was taken up into heaven. It is the beginning of the amazing story of how the Christian faith spread from a small band of fishermen and housewives in ancient Jerusalem to reach all around the entire world.

However, to call the book of Acts—or the whole New Testament, for that matter—a good story, is NOT to say that it isn't true. Or that it didn't really happen. Or that it was all just made up. No way.

The New Testament, unlike the Old Testament, was written down VERY soon after the events it describes. In this way, it is uniquely reliable. The earliest accounts were written just fifty years after the death and resurrection of Jesus, and the entire New Testament was completed by A.D. 100. That means that at least some of the people reading some parts of it actually could have BEEN there! There is no way the authors would have risked telling anything but the truth, the whole truth, and nothing but the truth to the very best of their memory.

It would be nice, of course, to say that we had all of the original manuscripts. Paul's letters written in Paul's own hand. But we don't. No more than we have the original manuscripts for the writings of Homer or Plato or Aristotle. We are talking about things that were written thousands of years ago! We DO, however, have a fragment of papyrus (an ancient form of paper) with a few verses from the New Testament written on it that is dated to A.D. 125, just twenty-five years after it was written! And we have a complete copy of the major New Testament writings dating from A.D. 175 to 250. That's not bad when you consider that scholars of ancient literature accept as "authentic" a COPY of a manuscript that is dated 300 to 1,500 years after it was originally written. Compared to all other ancient texts the authenticity of the Bible really is beyond dispute. The words of the New Testament are words you can rely on.

Use Your Imagination

Hello! Are you still there?!?

If—after getting all comfortable and settled in to read— you started to fade as we began talking about the kinds of issues and characters and stories that are in the Bible, then you are experiencing one of the biggest problems a lot of people have when they first try reading the Bible. It is what I call the SLEEP PROBLEM: as soon as you start reading, all you want to do is sleep. I am convinced this is because people EXPECT the Bible to be boring.

How silly.

The Bible is God's own book. And God is a lot of things. Boring is not one of them. Picture that first snowfall of the season, big fluffy flakes and bright sunshine, hats and mittens pulled out of mothballs, sleds brought down from the rafters, the blast of wet coldness that hits you like a snowball that has found its mark and wakes you up and makes you feel alive. Picture an evening in a funeral home, relatives embracing, children racing through the legs of their suddenly tolerant elders, smiles breaking out through tears. Picture the universe . . . which of course you can't because it is so vast, so unknowable, so full of silent promise. Consider how it teases us into faith in a Being bigger than ourselves. Who else could have stirred into existence something so amazingly complex as the universe? These things, all of them and more, are God's doing. Boring? I don't think so. Why would God's book be any different?

If you open up any old encyclopedia and look under *B*, it will tell you that the Bible is one of the most famous pieces of literature in the world. Literature, art, and drama have been more influenced by the words of the Bible than any other written work. You can read the Bible in more languages than any other book ever published.

What the encyclopedia will not tell you is that the Bible has changed people's lives. It is, today, changing the lives of some of the most important and powerful people in the world and of people you might walk right by and not notice. The Bible is changing my life, and maybe it is changing yours too.

Through the stories it tells, the Bible introduces you to a God who is loving and powerful and alive. You see God in action, parting the Red Sea[3] and raising the dead to life.[4] You hear the very voice of God, proclaiming liberty to the captives

[3]Exodus 14
[4]John 11:17-44

and comfort to the sick and hope to the brokenhearted.[5] How could you meet this living God without being changed?

Just in case it wasn't enough, however, to meet the almighty God in these stories, the Bible gives you a bonus. Through the stories it tells, you meet another very important person. You meet yourself.

I have seen myself clearly in the mistake-making Peter[6] and the running-for-his-life Elijah[7] and the angry-as-hell Martha.[8] I have seen myself, sinful and embarrassed and out of options, like the woman at the well.[9] I have seen myself, embraced and forgiven and given a second chance, like poor doubting Thomas.[10] The stories of the Bible are not just about a bunch of people long ago dead. They are about me and my life. They are about you.

When you sit down to read the Bible, expect the best. Expect to be moved to tears and filled with hope and caught off guard by laughter. Expect to be surprised and challenged and inspired and encouraged and changed. Expect to hear a LIVING God speak to you about the issues and concerns and fears and needs in your life.

As you are getting ready to spend some time reading your Bible, wait just a minute before you open it. Ask God, right in that moment, to show you something YOU really need to see. If you open the Bible, then, with a few basics under your belt and your imagination fired up and raring to go, I guarantee you won't find yourself falling asleep.

[5]Isaiah 42:1-9 and Luke 4:16-21
[6]Luke 22:54-62
[7]1 Kings 19:1-18
[8]Luke 10:38-42
[9]John 4:1-42
[10]John 20:19-29

GETTING INTERESTED?
Some Reading You Can Do

- **Proverbs 2:1-8** In this reading from the Old Testament, King Solomon—the wisest man who has ever lived— explains the importance of reading the Bible and valuing the Word of God. What does he say God's Word can do for you?
- **John 6:66-69** Here in this New Testament passage, the disciples say what people have been thinking for centuries: Jesus' words give us eternal life. He tells us things that can enrich our lives today and forever. How are you hoping the Bible will enrich your life?

GETTING PERSONAL:
Some Things to Think About

- What are you hoping to gain by developing a Bible reading habit? What are your goals on this new spiritual path you are taking? Write your goals down in your journal.
- What are you afraid of as you begin this new adventure? Change? Boredom? Disappointment? Confusion? Challenge? Say a small prayer right now, asking God to be with you as you take the plunge.
- Who do you know who might be asking the same questions you are? Make a list of their names. Do you think one of them might be willing to walk this path with you? Get on the phone right now and ask them!

GETTING SERIOUS:
A Bible Verse to Memorize

With all your heart you must trust the LORD and not your own judgment. Proverbs 3:5 CEV

chapter 4

Expect the best

Regular Bible reading is essential to an energizing spiritual life. So is prayer.

One of the reasons that reading the Bible leads to spiritual growth is that reading the Bible leads you into a life of prayer. In the stories of the Bible we meet a God from whom we can expect a response when we pray. And, in prayer, we meet God.

Fearful Times

Now, personally, I've always had high hopes. But even at the age of nine it was clear where my body was headed. It was never going to reach gracefully skyward. I never really had a nickname but, if I had, it surely wouldn't have been "Twiggy." None of my relatives ever tried to fatten me up because I looked like a bean pole. And it might have bothered me except I didn't really know what a "bean pole" was. Still don't. But I always knew that riding a sleek thoroughbred to victory in the Kentucky Derby was not in my future. Nor would I ever have a spot with the Harlem Globetrotters.

But, God help me, I did want to be Cher.

She was strong and independent and smart. She was a WOMAN. And every time she flung that long, black hair over her shoulder, I felt my own confidence surge. "I can do anything!" the Cher voice in my own head told me; "the world is mine!" It wasn't just that I was young and hopelessly naive. It was a time when girls all over were seeing visions and dreaming dreams.

"When I grow up," I asked my dad one day, "can I be the president?"

"Honey," Dad said, "you can be anything you want to be."

Sonny was a side dish to me. Colorful but nonessential. The only time I thought he really mattered was when they sang their signature song together, the all-time ode to confidence "I Got You Babe." No matter what else I might need but don't have, I got you and life is good. Dreams come true. Nothing can hold us back. Oh, what an era it was! Dr. King had a dream. Neil Armstrong planted our flag on the moon. And there was NOTHING Evil Kneivel couldn't jump over. In spite of all the disappointments we had shared and all the tragedy we had endured, we still believed that anything was possible.

Today, Sonny's widow is a congresswoman. Cher is selling exercise videos. And every Sunday night, along with the rest of America, I watch *The X-Files:* "Trust no one." Fear everything. Some of us will be watching it in syndication for at least the next decade.

Fear is the descriptive word of our time. Surveys show that most people today expect Social Security to be broke by the time they reach retirement age. We expect fifty-one percent of our marriages to fail. We elect our public officials based largely on the promises they make, but we don't really expect those promises to be kept. This generation is the first in American history to expect a lower standard of living than their parents enjoyed. At a time of unprecedented economic health and stability, the U.S. savings rate is still ten percent lower than it is in most other industrialized countries. Why? Well, is it possible that people only save for a future they really believe they'll have? We are people united, not by our dreams, but by our lack of them.

Expect Great Things

This *X-Files* generation can't be blamed for scoffing when encouraged to expect great things from prayer. We don't expect great things period. But the Bible tells us—and it is my experience—that there is, in fact, no more powerful thing a person can do than pray. Praying is what Daniel was doing that night in the lions' den.[1] It's what Paul and Silas were doing as they sat in a prison cell; God answered them with an earthquake that literally broke open their jail and set them free.[2] Jesus did it before he chose his disciples, when faced with temptation, when tired and in need of renewed strength, when surrounded on all sides by enemies. Pretty much all the time. It's what he was doing the night before he saved the world.[3]

It is interesting to note that very rarely does the Bible tell us what these people were saying as they prayed. There is no prescribed formula that we are given to follow, no template we're supposed to pull up and use to fill in the blanks. There are no "right" words assigned to the task. This means, of course, that there are no "wrong" ways to do it, either. And don't let anyone tell you otherwise. The last thing a drowning swimmer needs is someone telling him he's doing the front crawl all wrong. Just swim for your life! Don't worry about your form.

Prayer is a wonderfully individual experience. I do it best in the shower. It's something about the water rushing over me, as

[1]Read all about it in Daniel 6:1-23. And no, the lions didn't eat him.
[2]Acts 16:16-40
[3]Luke 22:39-46

clean and renewing as a baptismal shower. It makes me feel glad to think that I'm the child of a God who is so very eager to hand out second chances. The car is another place I have found myself talking to God. Often I do this out loud, figuring my fellow commuters will think I'm singing along with the radio. And usually I use very ordinary language. It isn't that I see God as a friend, exactly. At least, not all the time. I am too often completely mystified by something God has done or something that has happened for which I can find no other explanation than God. Sometimes I am just really mad at God and, at those moments, I don't even want God to be my friend. I use ordinary language mostly because that is the only language I own. My words come spontaneously, driven out of some hurting or happy or haunted place within me. I just talk. Formal prayers are useful mainly when I can't find any words of my own to use. I dread those times but I am thankful for those prayers. The "Hail Mary" sprang from my childhood to get me through a blinding snowstorm one scary night on my way home for Christmas break. And I can always manage to choke out the "Our Father" at funerals even when all other words have failed me.

There really is no right or wrong way to pray. In fact, the only mistake you could make would be to expect nothing to happen when you do it.

I remember a cover story in *Newsweek,* of all places, highlighting how often we expect too little and how silly we look when we do that. It was a special edition called "Beyond 2000: America in the 21st Century" and it was filled with predictions about the technology, foreign affairs, medicine, recreation, and so on of the future. Tucked inside these optimistic pages was a little article that tried to put all of these predictions into perspective. When, in the past, we have tried to look ahead, we often have not expected enough. In 1962, for example, somebody remembers Decca Records dismissed a new rock group predicting: "We don't like their sound. Groups of guitars are on their way out." They were talking about the Beatles, of course.

In 1977, the president and founder of Digital Equipment Corporation, Kenneth Olson, said: "There is no reason for any individual to have a computer in their home." And, in 1927, Harry M. Warner of Warner Brothers asked, "Who the hell wants to hear actors talk?" Sometimes, what our low expectations reveal is nothing more than a sorely underdeveloped imagination.

In my own life, if I'm not careful, my prayer life can be reduced to things like, "Please, God, just help me get through this day!" Or, as I'm pulling up to any one of the many occasions we have for family get-togethers, "Please help us all get out of this without killing each other!" Or simply, faced with one crisis or another, "Oh, God!" I know I'm not alone. So many people pray these kinds of "prayers," there is actually a term used to describe them. They're called "foxhole prayers." Prayers of desperation shouted at the universe in the hopes that someone, somewhere will hear. Personally, I have never visited a foxhole. So I prefer to call these "parking lot prayers." As in: "%@&!#* it, God, I'm late! I don't have all day to find a parking space!" This is not a prayer life. And these are not really prayers. They are wishes.

The difference between praying and wishing is this: Praying depends on God. Wishing depends on luck; and luck is unreliable. Just ask the guy who won $16.2 million in the Pennsylvania lottery a few years back. Since then, if I have the story right, he was arrested for assault, his sixth wife left him, and his brother was convicted of trying to kill him. Think twice about putting your faith in luck. God, on the other hand, promises great things when we pray. If the Bible tells us anything about prayer, it is this: Don't waste it! Pray for something WORTHY of the powerful, almighty, and ever-living God. Be clear. Be specific. Be outrageous. And expect something amazing to happen when you do it.

The apostle Paul, for example, is famous for the outlandish things he expected from God and from God's people. When addressing family issues in his letter to the members of the first-century church in Ephesus, Paul told husbands and wives to "Honor Christ and put others first."[4] Now, maybe this doesn't sound like a big deal to you, but back then, wives were less valuable than cattle. Later on in the same letter he asks the same mutual respect to grow between children and fathers and, unbelievably, between masters and slaves! Poor Paul has something of a bad reputation in certain circles today, because of his supposed anti-women sentiments. In fact, as you read this letter to the Ephesians, you meet a guy who was—for having lived two thousand years ago—positively enlightened! He asked for things that no one in his day was even dreaming about. He asked for things worthy of a great and mighty God, a God whose "power at work in us can do far more than we dare ask or imagine."[5] Sustained by his confidence in a God who can do wondrous things for us, Paul faithfully and courageously faced disappointment, rejection, imprisonment, loneliness, and betrayal. He expected God to do great things for him! Do you?

Expect God to ANSWER

For people who are so technologically astute, we can be pretty stupid sometimes. In fact, it is the technology itself, that evidence of our vast and wondrous intelligence, which sometimes leads us into doing or saying stupid things. For example, it always amuses me when I answer the telephone and the first thing I hear is not the expected, "Hi, is Emma there?" (The most frequent phone greeting we get now that our daughter is a teenager!) Instead, the caller—the person who MADE THE PHONE CALL in the first place—says in a startled voice, "Oh, I didn't expect anyone to answer!" Between the almost universal use of answering machines and a culture-wide busyness, we

[4]Ephesians 5:21 CEV
[5]Ephesians 3:20-21 CEV

often find ourselves making phone calls without expecting an answer.

That is also how we sometimes pray.

The first great thing that we can and should expect from prayer, however, is simply this: Expect God to ANSWER. In all the stories that are told about him, Jesus is never caught ignoring anyone who called upon him for help. Oh, he might have argued with them a little about whether or not they really needed what they thought they did. But he never just ignored people. It didn't matter how tired or worn out he was. He responded even when he was distracted or distressed. At one point, in fact, Jesus was especially upset. He had just been told that his cousin John had been murdered by King Herod. He went away to a "deserted place" by himself to pray, I guess, and to pull himself together. But a crowd of people followed him, wanting him to teach and heal them. When Jesus saw them, the story goes, he "felt sorry for them." Instead of coping with his grief in private, he spent the whole day ministering to them.[6] Jesus was ALWAYS there when he was needed. In fact, he came right out and made this promise: "Everyone who asks will receive, everyone who searches will find, and the door will be opened for everyone who knocks."[7]

Now God, being God, doesn't always answer on our timetable. In almost the same breath, Jesus told his listeners to be patient and not to give up just because things do not appear to be happening. Be persistent, Jesus said, in prayer.[8] Hang in there while God goes to work. God WILL go to work. I don't know if Jesus knew how hard this would be for us to do. Even if we manage to go into prayer confidently, expecting an answer, waiting is another story.

[6]Matthew 14:13-21 CEV
[7]Luke 11:10 CEV
[8]Luke 11:5-8

We don't like to wait for anything. One of the fastest growing markets in the food industry today seems to me, anyway, to be the one that produces prepared foods. It's hard to know what to make of a people who eat their salads out of a bag, dressing and croutons and all. BBQ now comes in a bucket in the refrigerated section of your local grocery store. And, at the meat counter, some chef somewhere has taken that chicken breast and already magically turned it into chicken kiev. Just heat and eat. It is the need for immediate gratification gone mad. Not long ago in the jobs section of my local newspaper, an article appeared titled "Bad Bosses." The advice to readers everywhere afflicted with such a problem? Find a new job. We are not a patient people. We know what we want, and even if we can't afford it we won't wait longer than it takes to pull out a credit card to buy it.

In contrast to contemporary impatience, there is a character in the Bible who illustrates clearly the kind of confident and persistent prayer that Jesus encourages. His name is Jairus. He was a leader in his community, a man used to being in control and doing things his own way. But, when we meet him, Jairus is desperate. So desperate he is willing to do things God's way. You see, his little daughter is sick. In fact, she's dying.

Jairus fought his way through the crowd to get to Jesus. He begged Jesus "repeatedly," the story says, to come with him and do something to heal his daughter. And Jesus, right away, went with him. But as they were going, a "large crowd followed Jesus" and pressed in on him, blocking his way, making demands, slowing him down. One woman, who had been hemorrhaging for twelve years, held onto the edge of his cloak until she was healed. Half a chapter later, we finally get back to Jairus. It must have felt to him like decades had gone by, eons. And then, some people came from his neighborhood and told him to forget it all. "Go home, Jairus. It's too late. Your daughter is dead."

If ever there was a moment to call it a day, to throw in the towel, to go home and cry yourself silly, this was it. Instead Jesus said, "Do not fear, only believe." Even when Jairus was ready to give up, Jesus didn't. Finally, Jesus arrived at Jairus's home and found the girl and healed her. She got up and had breakfast. Jairus, I imagine, embraced his daughter and felt the warmth of life in her and cried thankful tears. I'd be willing to bet he vowed never to expect too little, never to give up too soon again.[9]

Do you know what it's like to be at that point, where everything looks hopeless? Where God seems to live across some silent wasteland? Where you can't think of a single reason not to quit? I do.

Just six months after we were married, my husband and I were ready to give up. Instead, we went to counseling. Our counselor's name was Nick. One anguished night, Tim walked out of our apartment. He said he needed more space. For all I knew, he was gone forever. Years later, I found out what really happened. He drove around for awhile, praying. Finally, he stopped at a pay phone and called Nick. The advice that God gave him that night, through Nick's words, sent him back to our apartment and back to our marriage. It kept him there through all of the turmoil of those early years and through the boredom that came at the onset of these middle years. It has kept him here through career crises, midnight feedings, in-law struggles, financial uncertainty, and graduate school nightmares. I am betting it will keep him here through empty-nest anguish, retirement regrets, old-age crabbiness, and nursing home loneliness. Right up until the end. Nick's advice was simple. "Whatever you do," he said, "don't leave." Don't leave. Hang in there. Trust God to come through.

[9]Luke tells this story in 8:40-56.

Whatever it is you are praying about these days, DON'T GIVE UP. No matter how hopeless, how desperate, how alone you feel. HANG IN THERE. God will bless all your struggling, all the giving, all the forgiving, all the sacrificing, all the truth-telling, all the temptation-resisting. God will not leave you, ignore you, or disappoint you. God hears you. God will answer. Count on it.

Expect GOD to Answer

Of course, God's answer is not necessarily always the answer we were hoping for. I don't even want it to be! We can't be blamed, I don't think, for praying from our own perspective; it's the one we know the best. But what we are praying for is not always what is best for us. We can't even always know what that is.

Sometimes what we think is best for us is exactly the opposite. We have spent, for example, the past fifty years fighting forest fires. Smokey the Bear was a regular in my classroom growing up and his are the first TV commercials I really remember. But Smokey was just the beginning. We have developed a powerful system of brave men and women, armed with old bombers, trucks, helicopters, and up to a billion dollars a year to keep forest fires under control across the country. We have done such a great job, in fact, of putting out every little brush fire that the brush has been piling up for decades. Our

Only God can really see the big picture.

national forests are now so filled with dangerous, dry kindling that the fires get bigger and more unmanageable every year. Our strategy of fighting forest fires has worked so well that we have put our forests in unspeakable danger. We got what we wanted, all right. We did what we thought was best. And now we know, we were wrong.

When we pray, we had better be prepared for GOD to answer. God's answer is always the best—a truth I am counting on—but it is not necessarily the answer we were looking for.

One of the most famous "unanswered" prayers in the Bible belongs to Jesus' friend Peter. Jesus had just finished telling his disciples that the road ahead of them was a difficult one. "I am going to Jerusalem, guys," Jesus said, "not to become king . . . but to be arrested, betrayed, tortured, and put to death. That's the plan. Just thought you should know." But Peter wanted nothing of the sort. This was his teacher! His friend. And he couldn't see the big picture. He didn't even know there was a big picture. "God would never let this happen to you, Lord!" he said.[10] Now, Jesus actually gets a little ticked off with Peter at this point, probably because Jesus couldn't have been too excited about this whole death thing, either. The last thing he needed was more temptation not to go through with it. But you can't fault Peter for trying. He didn't know any better. He couldn't see the big picture. And that's the point.

The Bible reveals a God who does better than our best hopes. This is a God who listens, a God who cares. This is not a tame God, a pet God we can manipulate into granting wishes. Instead we have a God we can trust to answer our prayers with our absolute best interests at heart, and the big picture (which we cannot see) in mind.

I can remember when Chicago's famous Cardinal Bernadin announced his cancer was terminal. He had been praying for healing and worked hard for it, doing everything his doctors told him to do. His reward, it seemed, was a clean bill of health given to him in mid-August. But by the first of September, the doctors reversed their evaluation. He had less than a year to live.

[10]Matthew 16:22b CEV

In the flurry of media moments that followed, the cardinal acknowledged there would be some dark and difficult days ahead. He never minimized the anxiety and pain of the condition he shared with so many others. But he assured us all that he was at peace. In fact, he called his cancer a "special gift" from God. He believed it would give him a unique opportunity to teach and to lead. And, in fact, the way the cardinal faced death taught many of us more about life than anything else he had ever done. Being told that his cancer was back was not the answer to prayer he had hoped to hear. But knowing the impact he had on the lives of so many people, the cardinal would probably say that the answer he did get was even better.

When God's involved, it always is.

GETTING INTERESTED?
More Reading You Can Do

- **Psalm 8** The psalms are actually songs, written by God's people thousands of years ago. And you could read any one of several dozen of them that begin the same way— anguished—and end up proclaiming the power and faithfulness of God. Every human emotion is found within the psalms, every imaginable desire, every fear, every hope. We are assured, as we read, that God is okay with us making demands and assuming that we know what's best. But, in the end, these psalms all agree: The best answer to every prayer is whatever answer God provides. Try writing a psalm of your own that best sums up what you're dealing with right now.
- **1 Corinthians 1:18-31** God's people have always doubted, at least once in awhile, whether or not God really knows what he's doing. Paul addresses those doubts in this passage. What doubts do you have? Talk about them with a friend. Try talking about them with God.

GETTING PERSONAL:
Some Things to Think About

- When was the last time you spent more than a few minutes with God in prayer? Unless you give it more time than that, you're probably doing all the talking. Be quiet. And spend some time today just listening.
- Make a list of the things you can really count on. Put God on that list. Now, make strengthening your relationship with those people and your commitment to those things a top priority.
- Start a prayer list. Put it on your refrigerator, in your daily calendar, or some place else you will see it often. Keep a prayer list (instead of a wish list), including four different kinds of prayers:
  Prayers of adoration, for expressing your awe and delight in a great God.
  Prayers of confession, for admitting specific ways you need God's help and forgiveness.
  Prayers of thanksgiving, for answers given and blessings received.
  Prayers of request, for asking God to attend to your needs and the needs of others.

GETTING SERIOUS:
A Bible Verse to Memorize

Always be joyful and never stop praying. Whatever happens, keep thanking God because of Jesus Christ. This is what God wants you to do. 1 Thessalonians 5:16-18 CEV

chapter 5

The Liver Incident

Right up there with Bible reading and prayer in developing a strong spiritual life, there is this: Sharing. Giving. Doing for others. Jesus talked about this issue more than any other. It must be pretty important.

You've heard of all the other great showdowns, those moments in history when two powerful forces meet head on and do battle until the bitter end: the battle of Waterloo . . . Custer's last stand . . . Gettysburg.

But you haven't heard of The Liver Incident. Until now.

I was, I think, about five.

And I hated liver. This was not just a mild dislike. This was an "I'm gagging and I think I'm going to die" kind of dislike. This was a "There is no way in the world you can make me eat this, not even if you make me sit at this kitchen table until the rest of my class is graduating from high school" kind of dislike. And the worst thing was: Mom knew it. I know she did.

We were going to leave for my grandma's house after dinner. This was supposed to motivate me, I guess, to do the unthinkable. Which was to EAT the liver sitting there sneering at me upon my plate. But there was just no way under the sun that was going to happen. Everybody else finished before I did, naturally, BECAUSE I WAS NOT GOING TO EAT IT! "Now, you clean your plate, young lady," my mother said as she went off to finish getting ready to leave.

As soon as she was out of sight, I picked up my plate, scooted over to the garbage can, and scraped that disgusting piece of meat out of my life forever. Until, that is, she found it there.

"That was quick," she said when she came back in the room. "Did you eat that liver?"

"Yes, Mom, I ate it," I lied.

Needless to say, I did not make it to Grandma's house that night. But I did get THE LECTURE. Remember this? "You should be thankful you have food on your plate at all, young lady. There are children starving in India." Back then, my thought was, "Well, go ahead and send it to them. I don't think they'll like it either!" But now I know my mom was right. I was fortunate to have food on my plate at all. Even if it was liver.

God Blesses Us with Abundance

I believe that, like Mom, it is God's hope that we would look around at our lives and see how really blessed we are.

This is not something, by the way, that our culture makes it very easy for us to do. Our whole economy depends on you and me being forever dissatisfied with what we do NOT have.

That is why the mall is not a place I hang out very often. When I do, watch out. Before Christmas last year my husband and I took a day and went shopping together. We were astounded by all of the things we NEEDED that we never knew we needed before. Like brass Christmas stocking holders, for example. I mean, what are we SUPPOSED to do? Hang our stockings over the fireplace with plain THUMBTACKS? Then, of course, once we had shiny new brass stocking holders, we couldn't be expected to hang up our raggedy old stockings on them. We needed new ones. Quilted. In colors to match our decor. That led to a new Christmas tree skirt. And new ornaments. And . . .

You get the picture.

Our culture leads us into a place of continual discontent. But GOD'S PEOPLE, throughout the ages, have given thanks for whatever they had. Suffering persecution, without friends, and fearing for his life, the missionary Paul wrote: "Whatever happens, keep thanking God because of Jesus Christ. This is what God wants you to do."[1] Notice that he doesn't qualify this. He doesn't say be thankful when everything is going great and the sun is shining and your boss knows how lucky she is. He says, simply, be thankful. Always. Sometimes, of course, you have to look twice—or twenty times—to find something to be thankful for. But it's there.

God's people, forever, have been thankful people. As a young shepherd boy, not wealthy by any measure, living in the kind of constant danger that comes from working alone in the wilderness, David sang: "you fill my cup until it overflows."[2] Those words are from Psalm 23. It's too bad everybody thinks that psalm is only for funerals. The psalm is really talking about how great life is when God is in it. It looks us right in the eye and shouts: "Look at what you have, friend. And see how rich you are!"

Put Your Riches to Work at Home . . .

God blesses us with material riches. More importantly, God blesses us with spiritual riches. We are showered with God's forgiving, unconditional love. Why does God do this? So that we can share what we have been given with others.

[1] 1 Thessalonians 5:18 CEV
[2] Psalm 23 CEV

The primary characteristic of the early Christian community was their LOVE for one another. They shared everything. Not one among them was in need. They left us their example to follow, and their words of encouragement: "Keep being concerned about each other as the Lord's followers should."[3] I believe God wants us to start right here. By loving and sharing what we have with our families, our friends, and our neighbors.

A mom who attended a parenting class we offered at our church awhile back was worried about her two oldest children because her attention was so focused on the needs of her youngest, a little boy who was born with a serious illness. The older two were growing up fast. That is, these little girls had to learn how

We have more than enough of everything to go around.

to share a little bit earlier in life than the rest of us did. At night, the littlest one would often get up and need his mom beside him. Everyone in the house would hear his cries and wake up. But the older two would never be scared. They had each other. They'd climb back into bed whispering words of mutual encouragement. They knew their mom loved them, but they also knew where their mom needed—in that moment—to be. They were willing to share her with their little brother. That mom didn't need to worry. There is plenty of love in her house to go around.

And that's how it should be. If any one of us has a problem, we all do. If any one of us has something to celebrate, we all do.

[3]Hebrews 13:1 CEV. Kind of an odd book in some ways, Hebrews is full of wonderful passages like this one. Chapter 13 gives a sort of random list of advice about how to live the Christian life; Ann Landers two thousand years ago.

That's what families . . . friends . . . neighborhoods . . . and churches are for.

I thought I was graduating from seminary to go teach people something. Actually, I was the one who was taught. I learned my first lesson on my very first day as a minister. It happened at the hospital, where I found one of the families of my congregation distraught over the just-pronounced death of a loved one. He had been fighting cancer for a long time. But the end, however long-expected, is never easy. I struggled like the novice I was to find something, anything, to say. And I left them promising to show up later at their house, hoping I'd have thought of it by then. When I got there, they were kind enough to open the door and let me in. It was then that I was greeted, not for the last time, by the smell of love. You didn't know it had a smell, did you? Well, it does. Freshly baked bread. Pie. Hamburger casserole. Meatballs. All of it delivered within hours of her husband's death, by people who knew how to share the love that they themselves had received.

I often hear people complain about sending our hard-earned dollars to overseas missions. "Let's do something good with it here at home first," they say. Well, that's partly true. This is where we should begin. Right here. Having been so richly blessed, we should be busy filling our homes and churches and neighborhoods with love and generosity and joyfulness.

. . . and Everywhere!

But, if we're going to listen to what the Bible has to say, we need to also hear that HERE is just a beginning. We can't be done until we're sharing THERE, as well: "Be sure to welcome strangers into your home. By doing this some people have welcomed angels as guests, without even knowing it."[4] Share, the Bible tells us, with the poor. The sick. The faithless. The ugly.

[4]Hebrews 13:2 CEV

The mean. Because God cares for all of them. Do not stop sharing until the love God pours into you, fills you up and over-flows, rolling right out your front door and down your street and across the world.

I know a woman who would just die if I told you her name. She is shy in crowds of people to the point of painful humiliation. But somehow she has brought more people in to visit our church than any other person I know. I don't even know how she knows so many of them. But she keeps inviting them. And they keep coming. She says this is easy for her because she loves our church. But I know it is because she loves people. She sees their hurt, their pain, their worry, their need. And she knows there is something here that can help them.

Those of us who have been so richly blessed are responsible for all those people out there who have not been. Jesus shocked everybody when he said: "When you give a dinner or a banquet, don't invite your friends and family and relatives and rich neighbors. If you do, they will invite you in return, and you will be paid back. When you give a feast, invite the poor, the crippled, the lame, and the blind. They cannot pay you back. But God will bless you and reward you . . ."[5] Most of us will never actually DO this. But we could try simply seeing ALL people the way Jesus saw them, as worthy of love and respect. We could share more. A lot more. We could share our money and our time. We could share the stories of our faith. We could share a smile.

We've all learned from Richard Simmons and Dr. Spock that "cleaning our plates" isn't really a very healthy practice. So my kids are off the hook on that one. And I would never dream of cooking liver for dinner, much less making them eat it. But I DO ask them to tithe. They give ten percent of their allowance away each week. They are learning how to share.

And they really are learning. As I was driving my son to a day at summer camp, I realized I had forgotten my wallet. That

[5]Luke 14:12-14 CEV

meant I didn't have the fifty cents I usually gave him to buy a treat at the canteen during free time. He was distraught. That's the best part of the day at summer camp! The part he looked forward to the most. Just before he completely lost it, I had an idea. "Hey, I bet we can scrounge up fifty cents in change right here in the car!" And we did. From between the seat cushions and under the floor mats. In fact, we found almost a dollar. We continued our drive to camp happy and relieved. "You know," I said as we drove along, as much to myself as anyone, "I just thought of something. Some families in the world only have fifty cents to feed them ALL for a whole day. And we just have it lying around the floor of our car." Ethan didn't say anything. But when I looked over at him, big tears were rolling down his six-year-old cheeks.

You see, Mom was right, darn it. We ARE blessed. In more ways than we can count. We have more than enough of everything to go around. Even Ethan knows that.

GETTING INTERESTED?
More Reading You Can Do

- **Philippians 4:4-13** Paul was in prison when he wrote these words. This is a good passage to read when you're feeling sorry for yourself because of something you DON'T have. What do you have to be thankful for today?
- **Matthew 25:31-46** Jesus is pretty clear about what our responsibilities are to those "strangers" in need. What can you do to help someone else this week?

GETTING PERSONAL:
Some Things to Think About

- Imagine that you are stranded on a desert island with no hope of rescue. (I know it's corny, but do it anyway.) What five MATERIAL things (not people, not pets) would you like to have with you? Be honest. There aren't that many, are there?

- Who in your little corner of the world can you help today? What friend, what neighbor needs you? How can you make a difference to a stranger today? At the end of the day, write down in your journal three things you did for someone else.
- Try tithing ten percent of your income this week. Figure out how much that would be—ten percent of what you make in one week—and give it away to a good cause. If you're not sure what to do with it, call up your church and ask your pastor. Or get on-line and do some research into a cause you care about. Find an organization with a good, solid reputation. Or visit a local service agency, like a home-less shelter or a food pantry. If it looks like they're doing a good job . . . give it to them.

GETTING SERIOUS:
A Bible Verse to Memorize

God can bless you with everything you need, and you will always have more than enough to do all kinds of good things for others. 2 Corinthians 9:8 CEV

chapter 6
The telltale trike

**Although the Bible tells the stories of many interest-
ing individuals, all of them were part of a community.
That is where real spiritual growth happens. But life
together can be a challenge. Without God, it would
be impossible.**

Many families have stories that are told around the table each
Thanksgiving. These are the stories that have entered the family
mythology, stories that help the family define itself. These stories usually begin with "Remember when . . ." and everyone
happily turns their attention to the teller, hoping this isn't
"their" story but rolling their eyes good-naturedly when it is.

"Remember when Great-Grandma tipped the picnic bench
over, sent her paper plate flying, and lost her wig?!?" someone
will say, conjuring up hysterical memories of our rather plump
but usually decorous matriarch. And then, the story about our
larger-than-life, always right, never-lost-a-fight grandfather:
"Remember when Grandpa went running through the neigh-

borhood chasing Godfrey (his daughter's new little puppy) with a rolled-up newspaper in his hand, yelling 'God . . . come here, God!'—swearing he'd kill him if he caught him?!?" And "Remember . . ."

"Yes, yes! I remember," everyone agrees, even those too young to have been there for the event.

There is a little story sometimes told about me. The story of a telltale trike. My mother tells it by way of explaining why I am the way I am whenever somebody complains about me, which they occasionally do. Well, not "they." Usually it's my brother making the complaint. The eighteen months that separate us has never been quite enough. "That's Kelly," my mom will say when the crabby, stubborn, little demon inside of me is acting up again. "I remember when she was about two and a half years old. She was outside on the sidewalk between our house and the neighbor's with her new, red tricycle. Suddenly I heard a terrible noise. I ran to the back door and there she was. Her tricycle was all tangled up and, apparently, she was having trouble getting it to work right. So, instead of coming in and asking for help . . . instead of patiently working at it until the problem was solved . . . she was just KICKING THE DARN THING down the sidewalk." Everyone always laughs at this story because it isn't just a story about something that happened thirty-five years ago. It is a story about now.

A Holy MESS

As a little kid, I learned the finger rhyme "Here is the church. Here is the steeple. Open the doors and see all the people." I have taught that little poem to my own children. It is cute. And it is fun to see small children get their fingers all tangled up trying to mimic their moms. But it is wrong. In reality, you can't see people inside the church. Because the church IS people. People like me. Which explains why it is so often such a holy mess.

Groucho Marx, I think, gets credit for having said something like, "I wouldn't want to join any club that would have me as a member." I could say the same thing about the church. I know what's wrong with me, one deficit after another. Just ask my brother. Or, better yet, take a second look at that mangled, tangled-up trike. But the church people let me in anyway. In fact, from the very beginning two thousand years ago, they let anybody in. Prostitutes, tax collectors, and all sorts of people that no respectable citizen would be caught dead with. Or alive, for that matter. But those early Christians couldn't help themselves. Jesus himself got into trouble for not being choosy enough about who his friends were; he's to blame for giving them this example to follow. The church has always been full of very ordinary, very flawed people. No wonder we fight with each other and make such a mess of things so often.

Lots of churches have eye-catching message boards out front now. That way they can get a little sermonette in while telling you what time worship is. But these message boards can mean trouble. A friend of mine rear-ended a police car while trying to read one whose message was just a bit too lengthy for its placement on a speedy thoroughfare. True story. These boards can also spell trouble when they seem to invite a response from passersby. One church put the title for next Sunday's sermon out there, in big block letters, asking all who would listen: "Do You Know What Hell Is?" In response some smart aleck, who was apparently familiar enough with this church to have an opinion, scribbled underneath: "Come hear our organist."

The church is people. And people are often insensitive to each other. Sometimes we are just plain mean. People can be selfish. People can be dumb. Jesus knew this better than anybody. He was so certain we would mess it up that he gave very specific instructions about what to do when it happens. When you get into a disagreement with another member of the community, Jesus said, don't even bother coming to church until you get it straightened out. Go make up. Forgive each other. Get over it.[1]

Jesus addressed the issue of how to deal with conflict in the community because he knew it was inevitable. You see Jesus had to wrestle with it himself. We all know about the opposition he faced from people outside of the community of his followers. But, did you know, he also faced it from within? When he told his disciples, for example, that he would have to die in order to fulfill his mission, Peter yelled at him.[2] A big fight broke out when the mother of two of Jesus' disciples, James and John, tried to get them promoted over the rest of the disciples.[3] When some parents tried to bring their little children to be blessed by Jesus, his boneheaded disciples tried to chase them all away; Jesus was angry and told them so.[4] That famous picture we've all seen of Jesus with little children scrambling up onto his lap was inspired by that story, although you don't see the pouting faces of the reprimanded disciples anywhere! And don't forget it was one of Jesus' best friends who turned him over to the authorities in an astounding act of betrayal that led eventually to Jesus' death.[5] The little community that followed Jesus around was anything but idyllic. There was, in fact, a lot of fighting going on. They weren't saints until we made them saints. When Jesus knew them, they were just a bunch of very ordinary human beings. And wherever there are people, there is going to be trouble.

That is why Paul had to write so many letters. You'll find them if you flip through the very last pages in your Bible. He wrote to the churches in places like Ephesus, Corinth, Thessalonica, and Philippi. Paul had started all of these

[1]Matthew 5:21-24
[2]Matthew 16:21-23; Mark 8:31-33; Luke 9:21-22
[3]Mark 10:35-45. They didn't get it.
[4]Mark 10:13-16
[5]John 13:21-30 and John 18:1-8

churches himself. He would come into a new town, get to know some locals, and settle down for a few years to teach people about Jesus. Once they seemed to have the hang of it, he would move on to another town and do the whole thing all over again. He would leave somebody in charge of each church and entrust them to carry on. But, inevitably, they would mess it up. They would start fighting about who should be the leader, how to worship, what to believe. As soon as Paul would find out about it, he would fire off a letter to try and straighten things out.

"You stupid Galatians!" Paul wrote.[6] Paul was especially upset with the Christians in Galatia because they were messing up the very core of his teaching, that we are "saved by grace" and loved by God as a gift. Not by anything we have done to earn or deserve it. This was one thing upon which, for Paul, there could be no compromising.

And, in his letter to the Corinthians, Paul pleaded with them to stop fighting. "My dear friends, as a follower of our Lord Jesus Christ, I beg you to get along with each other. Don't take sides. Always try to agree in what you think," he wrote.[7] In fact, we have TWO letters from Paul to these people in Corinth. They had all sorts of problems! Craziness, inconsistency, crabbiness in the church is nothing new. It has always been this way and, frankly, there is no reason to believe that in this world it will ever change.

I met a woman not long ago who hasn't belonged to a church in more than eleven years. That's how long it has been since she moved here from Ohio. Shortly after she moved in, she started visiting a church not far from her new home. One Sunday morning, after she had been visiting for several weeks, she mustered up the nerve to talk to the pastor. "I really like it here," she said. The sermons were pretty good and the music was excellent. People seemed sort of friendly, at a distance. But

[6]Galatians 3:1 CEV
[7]1 Corinthians 1:10-17 CEV

when she told the pastor where she lived, he said, "Oh, you can't come here. You need to go to _____ parish on the other side of town. That's the church for your neighborhood." So she quit going there. She has promised that she'll come to our church for a visit, give it another try. I'm crossing my fingers. But I'm not holding my breath.

It is easy to point to the really big ways in which the church has messed up. We could start and end with the INQUISITION. Or we could go on and add to that ignoble chapter in church history the Crusades, schisms, indulgences, the persecution of scientists, the misguided passion of missionaries, the historical justification of slavery and the denigration of women. And in fact, I meet a lot of people who will give me such a list to justify their conviction that "I'll never set foot inside another church. They're all just a bunch of hypocrites!" But for most of us, our own personal stories are all we need to prove the point that the church is a mess. Even those of us who hang in there week after week can tell about how some church or some pastor or some "so-called" Christian has let us down, hurt and disappointed us, scared us or pushed us further than we were ready and willing to go. Because, the truth is, the church IS a mess. It always has been.

From the beginning, the church has been full of people like me. I know, therefore, not to even bother asking myself, "Why do people in the church act that way?" The better question is, "With so many people like me in the church, by what act of God do we NOT do even more stupid things, more often?!?"

A HOLY Mess

In fact, this is the only explanation for how the community of faith has survived all these years. It IS an act of God. If I am the reason the church is such a mess, God is the reason the church is holy. Paul actually uses this word to describe the church when he says to his friends in far-off Ephesus that the church is "like a building with the apostles and prophets as the foundation and with Christ as the most important stone. Christ is the one who holds the building together and makes it grow into a holy temple for the Lord."[8] The actual word Paul uses there is the Greek *naos*, which translates into the "inner sanctuary," the holy of holies. This is the place where God meets God's people. It is God's presence, the Bible tells us, that makes the church a holy place. Messy or not.

Last spring I conducted a wedding for a couple that has really been through a lot. She is twenty-eight and never married. He is thirty-two and has five children, ages thirteen, eleven, and nine-year-old triplets, all of whom live with him. This was the third time their wedding had been scheduled. The first two times, his annulment didn't come through in time. This time, the THIRD time, they decided not to wait any longer. That's where I came in. As I walked with them through the premarital classes and got to know them, I came to really appreciate them for their courage, honesty, sense of humor, and hopefulness. I've never seen a couple work so hard just to get married. Her mother didn't mind him so much or his kids but she was worried about what a burden this huge, new family would be on her young daughter. His mother had been her grandchildren's surrogate mother for so long that she wasn't sure she could trust anyone else to do the job. And pretty much nobody was crazy about me. "Whaddya mean, a WOMAN minister? Is that allowed???" I started off the rehearsal by reassuring everyone that, yes, this marriage would be legal. Then I smiled as big as I could at them and was happy to see a few cautious smiles back. Finally, when the day came, I arrived at the chapel and put my vestments on. Then I went out to meet the rest of the family and make sure everything was on schedule. I didn't get far before I saw the kids standing in the back of the church, looking very handsome in their little tuxedos and matching

[8]Ephesians 2:20-21 CEV

dresses. And looking very nervous. I went over to introduce myself. "Hi," I said, "I'm Pastor Kelly." They all told me their names and ages and then one of the older boys asked, "Are you the priest?" I guess you could say that, I said. "Are you the one who's going to help our dad get married?" asked one of the triplets. Yep, that would be me. That's just what I'm going to do. Then one of the girls took my hand and looked at me with such wise and serious eyes that, for a moment, everything stopped and became clearer than it has ever been. "You are beautiful," she said.

You are beautiful. Those words have been bouncing around in my head, lifting my spirits ever since. Now, I'd like to think that she meant that I was beautiful. And maybe she did, a little. Children are not usually very discriminating. But you know what I think she really meant? I think she really meant that IT was beautiful. The fact that I was willing to help her dad get married. The fact that, because I was there, she knew that somehow God was there and a part of it all.

> ## If I am the reason the church is such a mess, God is the reason the church is holy.

Even the fact, I think, that I am a girl. Like her. And you know what? She was right. That is beautiful. There is nothing, in fact, more beautiful than the church when we get it right. There is nothing more wonderful than the community of God's people gathered together to sing and to learn and to share and to grow. There is nothing more holy. Messy or not.

Together, by God's grace, the church has done some wonderful things over the centuries. Public education and public health care both began with churches. Churches have provided sanctuary for people in all kinds of trouble in places around the world. Dr. Martin Luther King Jr. came out of the church. So did Dorothy Day and Mother Teresa. Today, churches are first on the scene with relief aid wherever there is a natural disaster, a famine, a war. There is nothing more wonderful than when, in spite of ourselves, we get it right and let God work through us.

A Given

The community of God's people is a holy mess. But beyond that, for God's people, community is just a given. That's how it has been from the beginning. Jesus never had to tell his friends to "go to church." They WERE the church. And they wouldn't have known how to do it any other way.

One of the very first things Jesus' followers did after he left them to carry on was to get a bunch of people together for dinner. They prayed together and "broke bread" together and took up a collection to help the poor. They were as devoted to each other in those early days as they were to God. They weren't looking for perfection. They were looking for protection. They were looking for the kind of encouragement they could only get from others who were walking the same path, facing the same challenges, wrestling with the same doubts and demons. It would never have occurred to any of them to try and do it on their own. They needed each other and they knew it. In each other they found their strength.[9]

Jesus knew it would always be so. That's why one of the very last things he told his disciples was this: "Now I tell you to love each other, as I have loved you."[10] Later, in that same chapter, after Jesus gives his disciples this advice, he warns them that they will need it. The world will hate you, he told them. They will make it difficult for you to keep your promises to me,

[9]Acts 2:37-47
[10]John 15:9-17 CEV

to hold on to your faith, to do the things you know I want you to do. Hang on to each other for dear life, he says.

For God's people, the church is just a given. We need each other. And we're stuck with each other. So we might as well love each other, the way Jesus told us to. Love each other even when you're crabby, Jesus said. Love each other even when you're wrong. Love each other even through your differences and your disappointments. And when you are faced with the least lovable characters of all—the outcasts, the sinful, the sick—welcome them. And love them most of all.

Like that grown-up kid with the telltale trike over there. The one eating her Thanksgiving turkey, with the embarrassed look on her face. Love the ones who least deserve it, most of all.

GETTING INTERESTED?
More Reading You Can Do

- **John 15:1-17** These words are among the very last Jesus ever spoke to his disciples. He was doing a sort of whirlwind final lecture, summing up everything he had tried to teach them. In so doing, he points them to each other and gives them a vision of the community they will never forget. How could a faith community be a blessing to YOU?
- **Colossians 3:1-17** Here Paul gives instructions for how members of the community should behave. He would not have needed to do this if they hadn't been misbehaving! Lucky for us, since it gave Paul the opportunity to show us a better way.

GETTING PERSONAL:
Some Things to Think About

- What is the worst story you can tell from your own experience about the church? Tell somebody. Get it out. And then ask God to help you forgive whoever it was that hurt you or someone else.

- One of the things that gets in the way of community is thinking, "I could never bring myself to care about THEM." Well, what is it that makes YOU unlovable? Be honest when you make this list. Ask God to give you a heart that is open to other people, especially the unlovable and difficult ones.
- Make a list of the things you expect from a church. Then go back and cross off the things that are unrealistic and unfair. Now, if you don't have a church, go look for one that can offer the things that are left. If you have a church already, love it more.

GETTING SERIOUS:
A Bible Verse to Memorize

Love the Lord your God with all your heart, soul, and mind. This is the first and most important commandment. The second most important commandment is like this one. And it is, "Love others as much as you love yourself."
Matthew 22:37-38 CEV

chapter 7

WARNING:
Crossroads

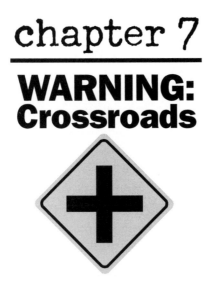

You start out reading the Bible. You end up a different person. That's what happens when you commit your life to following God.

You don't have to do much of anything to become a child of God. That's a given. In fact, you don't have to do anything at all. Jesus has already done it all for you. But once you are, and you know it, God has some pretty high expectations. So, here is fair warning, friend: If you're fixing to follow God, there are changes ahead.

I learned about this early on, too. My friends and I went exploring one summer day. Well, okay, I went exploring. They dared me to. The neighborhood gossip factory had decided that this particular house was haunted. It had been deserted for as long as any of us could remember, boarded up, and scary look-ing. I went in. There weren't any ghosts around that I could see but it was an awfully stupid thing to do. The floorboards looked like they might give way under an intruding mouse, much less me. I scrambled out as soon as I could and still save face with my friends. Of course, it wasn't them I should have been worried about. My mom was furious. "But, Mom," I said, "all my friends were there too." That's when I heard these words for the first time I can remember: "I don't care what all your friends do. You are MY daughter."

And that, I realized, made me different.

As followers of God, we are different from all the rest. God EXPECTS something of us. We are expected to listen to God, to take our cues from God's Word, to seek out God's advice and direction. We are expected to live our lives as though being a child of God MATTERS. And this is not always an easy thing to do.

What Do You Have to Lose?

First of all, it's not always easy to be a child of God when you have a lot to lose. You know that big crowd that was following Jesus? Well, no wonder! Jesus invited everyone to follow him. But he never tried to hide the truth about what following him would mean. Not everyone was willing to do it. Even today it is hard. It means making a change in the way you live, in what is important to you. Listen to what he turned around and told that big crowd one day: "You cannot be my disciple, unless you love me more than you love your father and mother, your wife and children, and your brothers and sisters. You cannot come with me unless you love me more than you love your own life."[1] What he meant is that if you are going to BE a follower of God, then nothing else can be more important to you than that. Yikes.

This would be no big deal, I suppose, to people who didn't have family or friends or beautiful homes or cars that started even in the winter. But what about for those of us who do?

[1]Luke 14:26 CEV

Those of us who have been blessed with many THINGS can get easily confused, forgetting WHICH thing is the most important.

I really admire people who can keep it straight. Awhile back, in an interview, the successful actor Denzel Washington described writing a check for a million dollars, more or less on the spur of the moment, to Nelson Mandela's foundation to help the youth of South

You are a child of God. And that makes you different.

Africa. Washington explained his action by saying, "You never see a funeral hearse pulling a U-Haul behind it."

Being a follower of God means, partly, being able to see past all the THINGS in your life to THE ONE THING that is most important. This isn't always easy.

The Crossroads of Life

Secondly, being a child of God is not easy when you come to a "cross-roads" in your life. That crowd following Jesus was probably as happy as could be. They were hearing great messages. Given his way with a few crumbs of food, they were never hungry. And I'm thinking nobody was ever sick for very long. But then there came that moment when Jesus turned to them and said: Choose. "You cannot be my disciple unless you carry your own cross and come with me."[2]

This moment of truth comes to everyone who wants to follow Jesus. A friend of mine who has just recently turned the corner from being a spectator to being a participant on the journey of faith described the moment when he knew it had happened. "I realized that I could no longer make any decision just

[2]Luke 14:27

because it was good for ME!" Now God is a part of his every
move.

The fact is, every decision we are faced with becomes a
crossroads of sorts. At every turn, we are faced with a choice.
Some of those choices are small ones. Do I shake my fist and
honk at that guy who cut me off or not? But sometimes the
choices are huge. Do I stay in this marriage, even though it has
gotten so hard? Or do I leave? Do I quit this job because I am
being asked to do things I know are hurtful to other people? Or
do I stay because the money is so unbelievably good? Do I make
a sacrificial gift to this organization I believe in? Or do I buy
that new car? Being a follower of God means that, when you
come to the crossroads, you go the way of Jesus. You go the
way of truth and courage. You go the way of compassion and
self-sacrifice. You do the right thing in everything. You lead
with love.

Facing Failure

Finally, being a follower of God is not easy when you fail. And,
if you choose to walk this path, you most certainly will. I walked
the "stations of the cross" at a Catholic retreat center not long
ago. This meant hiking a beautiful, wooded path and stopping
every so often to reflect upon a sculpture, hidden there among
the trees, depicting one of the events that occurred during the
last day of Jesus' life. This is what struck me: along the way to
Calvary, as he was carrying his cross, Jesus FELL DOWN three
times.

God asks a lot of those who follow him, so much so that
even Jesus fell down in the midst of trying to carry it out. You
will too. But what God asks of us more than anything else, I
think, is to stick in there with him. When you fall down, get
back up again.

This is the secret to success in our material lives. You know
that already. Henry Ford went broke five times before succeed-

ing. Walt Disney was fired by a newspaper editor for having a lack of imagination. Colin Powell was a poor student whose parents feared he would never make it. Success in life comes to those who refuse to let failure destroy them. When they fall down they get up, brush themselves off, and try it again. This is how it is in our spiritual lives as well.

I have seen people let all kinds of failures ruin their relationship with God. Failed marriages. Failed businesses. Failed dreams.

Don't.

Of all the things God asks of those who follow him, this is perhaps the most important. Finish it. Stick it out with him. Hang in there, even when it feels like you have too much to lose if you follow Jesus . . . even when you are faced with the tough choices being a Christian demands . . . even when you fail and fall off the faith wagon. Even when the sermons at church are putting you to sleep. Even when some spiritual person you trusted and admired turns out to be mortal and mistake-ridden just like everyone else. Even when your old friends are telling you they don't like this new self you have become since you let God into your life. Even when this new Bible-reading habit you've started doesn't seem to be having any kind of impact on you. Even when you are full of doubts. You are a child of God. And that makes you different. What was once "good enough" for the person you were isn't good enough for the person you are becoming.

Jesus warned the crowd that following him would not be easy. But he didn't tell them that to scare them off. He just wanted them to know what they were getting themselves into. If you were going to build a tower for example, or a house, wouldn't you sit down first and figure out what it was going to cost? Before you jump into following Jesus, don't you want to know what you're getting yourself into?[3]

[3]Luke 14:28-29

Jesus thought we should.

Jesus encourages us to be smart about our decision to follow him or not. We should know what we're getting into before we get on board. He won't try to fool us. Following Jesus will cost us something. Of course, what we gain is eternal and worth more than any sacrifice we might ever have to make. Just don't say I didn't warn you.

GETTING INTERESTED?
More Reading You Can Do

- **Philemon** In this little letter Paul writes to ask Philemon, a new follower of God, to make a tough choice: To welcome back his runaway slave, Onesimus, as a "beloved brother." Philemon, however, is not alone in having to make a choice. This letter was hand delivered by none other than Onesimus himself! What tough choice will following God require you to make?
- **Acts 5:12-42** The early Christians were faced with one hard thing after another. Through it all, God was there! How do you see God supporting you as you face the hard things in your life?

GETTING PERSONAL:
Some Things to Think About

- Is anything in your life getting in the way of your relationship with God? What are you afraid to lose? Is it really worth hanging on to? Make a list of the things you are afraid to give up. Ask God to help you get your priorities in order.
- Are you at a crossroads in your life? What choice is God asking you to make?

- Are you being tempted to give up . . . on your marriage . . . your kids . . . some commitment you've made at work or in a friendship or at church? Ask God to give you the strength and courage to hang in there. Make a list of the steps you can take today to help you keep your commitments.

GETTING SERIOUS:
A Bible Verse to Memorize

Christ gives me the strength to face anything.
Philippians 4:13 CEV

chapter 8

Pick Up Your Hoe

Through the Bible God speaks to us. Expect to be comforted. Expect to be challenged. Expect to be changed. But, listen, you should expect to have to work at it, too.

When it comes to searching for spiritual truth in the ancient stories of the Bible, no experience is necessary. None. I really meant that when I said it. But "no experience" is not the same as "no effort." The Irish have a saying: If you're going to pray for potatoes, you'd better pray with a hoe in your hand. If you really want to get to know God better, pick up your Bible. There's no way around it. You're in for some hard work.

Now, let me repeat myself for a moment by saying that God has made every effort to communicate with us in a way that we could understand. God's life is, in a way, an open book. Jesus promises: "So I tell you to ask and you will receive, search and you will find, knock and the door will be opened for you."[1] You could understand those words in a lot of different ways, but I think he was mostly talking about himself. If you go looking for God, God will find YOU. God doesn't play hiding games.

[1]Luke 11:9 CEV

This is not true about me. In fact, most of us are really good at hiding. We hide from the truth. We hide from each other. We even try, sometimes, to hide from ourselves. It all started when we were kids, remember?

My favorite outdoor game was a variation on the old hide-and-seek game called "kick the can." I was a master. I would find the very best hiding places, awful scary places, where no one would even think to look. And I would stay there until the bitter end. I was determined not to be found, and I wasn't. I missed supper that way a few times.

But God is not interested in playing hide-and-seek with us. God is not hiding out. God is in full view. We have been given a book about God, for goodness' sakes, which we can read with our own two eyes. God has made every effort to be found.

This is where we come in.

Reading the Bible and getting to know God better through the words written there takes effort. I've read the Bible—or some little part of it, anyway—just about every single day for the past fourteen years. Give or take a day or two. I've had to replace my Bible three times along the way because pages were falling out and they finally just wore out on me. And, you know, after all this time there is still stuff I don't understand. Ideas I struggle with. Stories I don't like. Passages that make me scratch my head and wonder what in the world God was thinking when these words were written. I hate the fact, for example, that God could get so mad at the world that Noah would need an ark in the first place.[2] And it scares me a little to hear Jesus say that he'll know how much we love him based on how well we take care of the hungry, the sick, and those in prison.[3]

It takes work on my part, thought and prayer and study and a willingness to look at myself honestly, to really get it. To

[2]Genesis 6–9
[3]Matthew 25:31-46

REALLY get it, I mean. To be changed by it. And I'm guessing that's what you're hoping for. To be changed.

You picked this book up in the first place because you want to know more about God. And probably because you want to KNOW God, in a personal, life-changing sort of way. But the fact is, if you want to know who God is, you're going to have to WORK at it. If you want a vibrant, adventure-filled, life-sustaining spiritual life, you're going to actually have to do something to get it. There really is no easy way to become a more spiritual person. No easy way to grow wise. No shortcut to the peace that passes all understanding.

It is possible. But you're going to have to pick up that hoe.

Now, Start Somewhere

Maybe you already have. But, just in case you haven't, it's time to crack open your Bible and get started. Whatever you do, though, don't start at the beginning! Anybody who has ever opened up to the book of Genesis—book one, chapter one, page one—and started reading knows that no matter how much of a running start you get, you are quickly bogged down in lists of family lineage, detailed instructions for building a temple, and pages of regulations on how to prepare dinner. This is all important stuff, in its own way, but save it for later.

I would suggest that you start with Luke. In his gospel, he is really trying to tell a story that makes sense and keeps you awake. He says so himself.[4] And then read Acts, which was also written by Luke. The gospel tells about Jesus' life. Acts tells about what Jesus' followers did after Jesus put them in charge. Luke is the blockbuster movie. Acts is the sequel. If you read these two books together, you get a pretty good picture of all the major events that occurred in the life of Jesus and right after he put his followers in charge.

[4]Luke 1:1-4

After that, you're on your own. Read whatever interests you. If you'd like to get a flavor for how REAL God's people are (and how real God is TO THEM), open up to the book of Psalms. Every imaginable human condition is represented in these poems and songs. Every conceivable emotion. Psalm 4 demands: "Answer me when I call, O God of my right!"[5] Psalm 40 gives thanks: "I waited patiently, LORD, for you to hear my prayer. You listened and pulled me from a lonely pit."[6] Psalm 60 complains: "O God, you have rejected us, broken our defenses; you have been angry; now restore us!"[7] Psalm 84 sings for joy: "Happy are those who live in your house, ever singing your praise!"[8] Read these psalms and you'll know there is nothing you could say to God that God hasn't already heard before. It'll free you up to be more honest with God than you have ever been.

And, if you're looking for something serious to chew on, turn to Paul's letter to the Romans. Paul was a scholar. Wrote like one, too. He wrote this particular letter to the Christians in Rome as a way of introducing himself and his faith to them before he dropped by for a visit. Unlike all of the other letters Paul wrote, that dealt with particular issues bothering the people he was writing to, the whole point of Romans is to explain what Paul believed. It may take awhile for you to figure out what he's saying in places. I expect to still be working on it forty years from now. His main point is summed up in the first chapter: "I am proud of the good news!" he writes. "It is God's powerful way of saving all people who have faith, whether they are Jews or Gentiles."[9] In other words, God loved us enough to send Jesus to save us. ALL of us. Keep referring to that as you read through the rest of his letter, and even the most confusing passages will be clearer.

[5]Psalm 4:1a NRSV
[6]Psalm 40:1-2a CEV
[7]Psalm 60:1 NRSV
[8]Psalm 84:4 NRSV
[9]Romans 1:16-17 CEV

The point is, read what interests you. If you're a sort of fun-loving, free spirit, try just opening up your Bible at random each day, and discover what God might have to say to you through the passage that catches your eye. If you need a bit more structure in your life, choose a reading plan. Read a book at a time. Or read the whole New Testament from start to finish. Or, go ahead, start at the beginning and work your way through to the end.

But read. Something.

Find a Method That Works for You

To really get something out of what you're reading once you've started—whether you're reading random passages every day or you're tackling one new book at a time—you have to be engaged in it. It's important to have a Bible you can mark up and scribble in, a book you can USE.

There are all kinds of methods people use to help them read and study the Bible. Some people find it helpful to keep a journal of their thoughts, prayers, and questions as they read. Some use a highlighting marker or a pen to underline passages and sections that are especially meaningful.

I have designed my own little key to use as I read. I use a variety of different symbols and put them in the margin next to passages that have hit me. This way I can remember WHY I highlighted something or another. It also helps me commit more of my reading to memory. Some of my symbols:

   ⌣ Made me laugh!
   > I really need to remember this
   ! This is a surprise!
   ??? What in the world does that mean?!?

I have a lot of other symbols, too. It's fun to make them up. Try it yourself. Or find some other method of Bible reading and study that works for you. There is no one right way to do it.

Don't Be Afraid to Look under the Hood

Somebody once told me in a stunning admission that he looked at his faith life the same way he looks at his car. He wants it to start when he gets in it. He wants to be able to drive it wherever he wants to go. And he wants it to be reliable, no matter how bad the road conditions or weather might be. But he doesn't want to have to look under the hood. I'm guessing he doesn't like to change his own flat tires, either, which is the first thing my grandfather made me do when I got my driver's license. The popularity of lube shops that look more like fast-food restaurants than garages tells me that my friend is not alone.

You could, I suppose, operate in your spiritual life the way my friend operates his car. You could let somebody else take responsibility for it—a spouse, a parent, a pastor—and hope they're around when you run into trouble. But I have been stranded on the side of the road with a broken-down car too many times (especially in the days when I held my cars together with duct tape) to want my spiritual life to end up in the same condition. I've chosen to take responsibility for my own spirit, to do MY part in sustaining a healthy relationship with the faithful and ever-loving God. The fact that you are reading THIS book tells me that you, too, have already made the decision to take a more serious approach to your spiritual life.

So, once you have started a Bible-reading habit, here is a suggestion for how to take it to the next level. When you read a story or a passage, first of all let God speak to you in that initial encounter. Ask yourself: what might God be trying to say to me right here, right now, through these words? Meditate on that a bit.

Then, go deeper. Search the text for clues to what the author was originally hoping to say to the people who first read these words. As you read, ask yourself these additional, key questions:

- Who is writing this? And when are they writing?
- Who is the author writing to? And why? What are issues these people were facing?

- What is this author trying to say? What is his or her main purpose or point?

These key questions will help you understand the historical context within which the story or passage was written. They will help you see what the author was trying to say THEN so that you can better understand what God is saying to you NOW. Keep these questions tucked inside your Bible and look for the answers as you read.

Often the answers to these questions can easily be found right in the story itself. For example, the gospel writer, John, explains toward the end of the book why he wrote his story down: "Jesus worked many other miracles for his disciples, and not all of them are written in this book. But these are written so that you will put your faith in Jesus as the Messiah and the Son of God. If you have faith in him, you will have true life."[10] John wants you to come to believe in Jesus through the story he tells and he is up front about it. Everything he writes and even the order in which he writes it is designed to bring you to a place where you say about Jesus, "I believe." Each of the four gospel writers—Matthew, Mark, Luke, and John—share this purpose.

On the other hand, Paul is writing letters. And he is writing letters to people who already believe in Jesus. He is writing to them about the issues they are facing as they try to live out their faith. He is encouraging, teaching, and challenging them. And he is answering their questions. In one place, writing to the Christians in Corinth, he actually says: "Now I will answer the questions that you asked in your letter."[11] Paul is writing about particular issues, facing specific communities, nearly two thousand years ago. Sometimes, what he writes seems strange to us. Old-fashioned. Irrelevant. Occasionally even offensive! But look deeper. Try to understand what Paul was saying back then. And

[10]John 20:30-31 CEV
[11]1 Corinthians 7:1 CEV

why. Then be open to what God might be saying to you, today, through Paul's words.

For example, Paul tells his friends the Corinthians that he never eats meat.[12] My would-be vegetarian daughter would very much like to use his words to justify our household becoming meat-free. But, in fact, Paul wasn't making a case for vegetarianism. He was talking specifically about meat being offered to idols. And he was saying that, even though as a Christian he was free to eat ANYTHING, he chose not to eat meat offered to idols because some people might misunderstand and assume that he was worshiping idols . . . instead of the God of Jesus Christ. He uses this situation to explain to his friends that, even though we are free to do whatever we want, we have a responsibility as followers of Jesus to set a good example for others.

Now, the last time I was at the grocery store, I saw beef and I saw pork and I saw chicken. I even saw *lengua,* which I knew was Spanish for "tongue." But I didn't see a section for "meat that has been sacrificed to idols" anywhere. This just isn't an issue for us today. But that doesn't mean Paul's words are meaningless. On the contrary, I have found them very helpful. For example, these words have helped guide my own view of alcohol. As Christians, our Lord has set us free from every kind of religious law. We are free, therefore, as the people of God through Jesus Christ, to enjoy alcoholic beverages in moderation. In fact, the Christian Brothers are not only great educators, they have a tradition of making fine wines. And it was the monks in Germany who first earned that nation its reputation for good beer. Jesus himself turned water into wine at a wedding so that the party could go on![13] But there are many people in our communities, in our families, and in our churches who struggle with alcohol addiction. And so, while we are free to use alcohol, we must do so carefully and sparingly, setting a good

[12] 1 Corinthians 8:13
[13] John 2:1-11

example at all times, and respecting the "temple" of our physical bodies as a gift from God.[14] Christians need to be especially sensitive to those who struggle, not using alcohol at all in the company of friends and family who are vulnerable.

It is important to take the historical context of each story and each passage into account when reading the Bible. Knowing what Paul—or any of the biblical writers—meant THEN helps us make sense—and make use—of what they mean NOW. It is important to think analytically about what the author is trying to say. This requires making an effort. It means looking under the hood.

Get Help

If you are feeling like this Bible reading is all of a sudden getting more complicated, you might want to consider, at this point, getting some help! In most bookstores where Bibles are sold, you can find a variety of resources to help as you learn to get around in the Bible and get something out of it.

One of the first decisions you'll have to make is which version of the Bible you want to use. Unless you are able to read ancient Hebrew or Greek, you will be using a translation. Scholars who are experts in ancient languages and cultures, who of course take their work very seriously, have prepared these translations.

The first translation of the New Testament from the original Greek into English appeared in 1525. It was done by a man named William Tyndale and, although eventually his translation became the standard for the English-speaking world, he was at the time considered a heretic and burned at the stake. It is a lot less dangerous to prepare a translation of the Bible these days. Maybe that's one reason there are so many different kinds of translations available!

[14]1 Corinthians 6:19

The most well known translation, probably, is the King James Version, published in 1611. For two and a half centuries it was the only "authorized" version in the English-speaking world. Being some four hundred years old, it sounds strange to the modern ear, using the formal *thee* and *thou*. It also is too old to take advantage of more modern discoveries and archeological finds that have helped clarify older translations. It is interesting from a historical perspective, but not recommended for average Bible readers today.

Some versions of the Bible today, such as The Living Bible, are more like paraphrases of the original languages. These are easier to read, which is a big relief if you've been trying to make your way through the King James Version, because MAKING it easy to read for people today was the translator's priority. But they can tend to wander away from the original Greek and Hebrew languages so far that the author's intention is lost and the translator's own biases show up.

My preference is for those versions that are written in contemporary English but that stick closely to the original languages. The NIV (New International Version), the NRSV (New Revised Standard Version), and the CEV (Contemporary English Version) are more recent translations that sound more or less like everyday English but that try faithfully to represent what the original authors wrote. They will even give you the literal Greek or Hebrew translation where they have chosen another way to say it.

Once you choose a version of the Bible, you'll want to decide what "extras" (if any) you want with it. You can buy a plain paperback Bible without any bells or whistles for under five dollars. Some Bibles have a thumb index, listing the name of each book and making it easier to find the passage you are looking for. Other Bibles, which I highly recommend, are called "student" or "study" Bibles. They include helpful information about each book and even each story, making it easier to under-stand the historical context of what you are reading. There are study Bibles for every group imaginable—women, men, couples, teens, busy people, and so on—that feature commentary and reflections of special interest to the people in that category. There are also Bible dictionaries and commentaries available for a more serious and in-depth understanding of the historical context and contemporary meaning of every biblical passage. A few of my favorites are recommended at the end of this book. The choice you make will be an entirely personal one based on your price range and your own special needs. There are tremendous resources available today to make Bible reading easier and more interesting. You can actually have fun choosing the resources that are best for you.

Personally, though, I have always found that the best source of help as I struggle to read and understand the Bible can be found in the face of a friend. Or two. There is no better way to really get something out of the Bible than to talk it over with others. Find a partner, if you can, or a small group of friends. Study the Bible together. Many churches have Bible studies that are open to newcomers, even to those who are not members. Visit a few and find one that's right for you. Or invite some people you know to start up a Bible study of your own. Oh, they might look at you funny the first time you suggest it. But my guess is, they are just as curious and just as much in need of "good news" as you are.

GETTING INTERESTED?
Some Reading You Can Do

- **Psalm 1** This lays it out pretty clearly: rooting yourself in God's Word leads to life! Make a commitment to root yourself through the habit of daily Bible reading. When and where will you read every day?
- **Matthew 7:24-27** Here Jesus uses the image of a house to describe the kind of life we have when we build it on him. What does your spiritual house look like now? What would you like it to look like?

- **John 1:1-14** The Bible is the written Word of God, and through the stories there God speaks to us. But God's Word is bigger even than the Bible. God's Word is ALIVE! Jesus is God's Word as "a human being" and so, everything we read in the Bible we interpret through what we know about God in Jesus. Jesus is the final Word!

GETTING PERSONAL:
Some Things to Think About

- Can you think of anything worthwhile that you have NOT had to work for? Write down the things in your life that are most important to you . . . your career? Your friends? Your classic car? Think about how much effort it takes to sustain these things!
- Now, write down your SPIRITUAL dreams. Do you want to feel closer to God? Lose your guilt? Discover your calling? Fulfilling these will take just as much work. Make a list of the things you are willing to do for the sake of your spiritual dreams. Will you read the Bible every day? Pray regularly? Participate in weekly worship with a community of God's people? Pledge to make a difference in the world by giving away a certain amount of your resources (time, abilities, money, possessions)? Make a habit of looking at yourself honestly, confessing your shortfalls and thanking God for your blessings.
- Make a plan for accomplishing the things you have committed to doing as you continue your spiritual journey. For example: write down your plan for daily Bible reading in your journal. What materials or resources do you need? Make a list and go get them.

GETTING SERIOUS:
A Bible Verse to Memorize

Show me your paths and teach me to follow. Psalm 25:4 CEV

afterword
One final thought

Keep at it.

My daughter has been after me to teach her to mow the lawn. We have just enough grass and just little enough time that we went out and bought one of those little riding mowers a few years ago. The closer my daughter has gotten to driving age, the more she has been wanting the feel of a wheel in her hands. I have been resisting. And not just because the thought of having a child old enough to drive sends me reeling with visions of myself in trifocals and support hose. But because I actually like to mow the lawn.

I like the way the lawn looks with a fresh cut and I like the sense of accomplishment I get from being able to see what I've done when I'm finished. I like knowing that my effort has helped make sure that this little corner of the world, at least, will not be overtaken by the weeds that would surely choke out the grass if I wasn't taking care of it. I like to mow the lawn even though I KNOW that, in a few days, it's just going to have to be done all over again. The sun will shine and the rain will fall and the grass, doggone it, just keeps growing.

This is true about a lot of things in life. We put in a good solid effort to make a difference somewhere, even though we know that at some point we're going to have to do it all over again. Because the work we're doing is never done. It's that way with housework and paperwork, marriage and friendship and child-rearing. It is that way, I think, with our spiritual lives.

Our work is never done.

I hate to tell you this, but you're not going to read the Bible in a weekend and wake up on Monday a completely different person. It just doesn't happen that way. You might come a little closer to knowing what God wants for you. You might experience God at work in you, melting your heart or healing your hurts or calming your fears or calling you into some new adventure. But then you'll turn around and feel like you're right back where you started. You won't be, of course. But you'll feel like it. We will—no matter how much Bible reading and prayerful living we do—always be, well, sinners. We'll have doubts. We'll get tired. We'll get bored. We'll wander away. Weeds will start growing. And we'll suddenly realize the grass needs to be cut all over again. Spiritual growth is not something that happens in a weekend. It takes a lifetime.

God will be there as you study and as you pray and as you do your best to live your life the way you know God wants you to. God will help you as you do it. God will bless your efforts.

Keep at it.

For Further Reading

- For answers to basic questions like, "Who is Jesus?" and, "Why bother about sin?"—questions you might be asking yourself as you read the Bible—look for *Christian Faith: The Basics* by Walt Kallestad, Augsburg, 1999. Call 1-800-328-4648 or go to www.augsburgfortress.org to order.
- For a closer look at the life of Jesus, read the inspirational *God Came Near: Chronicles of the Christ* by Max Lucado, Multnomah Publishers, 1998.
- For help getting acquainted (or reacquainted) with words that are part of the Christian vocabulary as you begin to make sense of what you are reading and hearing at this stage of your spiritual journey, read *Amazing Grace:*

A Vocabulary of Faith by Kathleen Norris, Riverhead Books, 1998.

- For a solid series of commentaries that will give you an in-depth look at each book in the Bible, look for the old but good Daily Study Bible Series by William Barclay, Westminster John Knox Press, 1979. Available from Augsburg Fortress at 1-800-328-4648 or www.augsburgfortress.org.
- A series of New Testament commentaries that may be helpful to you is Augsburg Commentary on the New Testament, from Augsburg Fortress.
- For a guide to daily Bible reading and prayer, try using the *Connection Planner*—available for adults, students, and early childhood. A fantastic resource available through the Bible League. Call 1-800-334-7017 for more information and to place an order.
- A daily resource for Bible reading and reflection designed for people new to the faith is a little devotional booklet called *The Word in Season,* available by subscription: 1-800-426-0115, ext. 639.